He Got Me Jazzed And Inspired

Emmanuel Elendu

Publishing

Copyright © 2017 by Emmanuel Elendu

He Got Me Jazzed And Inspired
By Emmanuel Elendu

Printed in the United States of America

ISBN-13: 978-1479390991
ISBN-10: 1479390992

All rights reserved. No part of this book may be reproduced, stored in retrieval system, or transmitted in any form or by any means: electronic, mechanical, photocopies, recording, scanning or other-except for brief quotations in critical reviews or articles, without the prior written permission of the publisher. This book or parts thereof may not be reproduced in any form, stored in a retrieval system, or transmitted in any form by any means- electronic, mechanical, photocopy, recording, or otherwise- without prior written permission of the publisher, except as provided by the United States of America copyright law. Unless otherwise noted, all Scripture quotations are from the New King James version of the Bible. Copyright © 1979, 1980, 1982 by Thomas Nelson, Inc., publishers Used by permission.

Cover Design By: Faith Walley

Published By:
Cibunet Publishing
P. O. Box 444
Woodlawn, NY 10470
Email: admin@cibunet.com
Website: www.cibunet.com

Table of Contents

ACKNOWLEDGMENT: 7

FOREWORD: 10
Jazzed & Inspired: My Story

CHAPTER 1: 15
Disclaimer: I write For Dummies

CHAPTER 2: 29
Faith: Nuggets For The New Life

CHAPTER 3: 53
The Play and the Practice

CHAPTER 4: 75
Develop a Thirst For Reality

CHAPTER 5: 89
My Purpose & My Poise

CHAPTER 6: ················103
Spiritual Victory

CHAPTER 7: ················117
Training For the Christian Worker

REFERENCES ················148

Acknowledgment

As a college student and member of The Christian Union (CU), I learned and indeed went through my first Bible College years while studying Agriculture. Discipleship program under CU was in-depth and all-round. I am forever grateful for the training I received from the fellowship and from Nigeria Fellowship of Evangelical Students and Scripture Union Nigeria. They all have a claim on God's touch in my life. The rich content, in-depth discovery of the WORD and insistence on purity, love, sacrifice and service cut across every sphere of our training in the camps and fellowships. I remember such slogans: 'For each and every day, you have no right to physical food until you have eaten the spiritual manna', and that kept us going. In fact, Scripture Union provided a platform for the expression of the things learned and we witnessed clean cuts across all social strata. There was a fusion of Christian values in diversity without regard to color, race or tribe. The rich, the poor and the middle class ate from the same plate.

    I have enjoyed unmatched support from my family. Their encouragement and prayers have sustained this effort. I owe my wife, Chinwe, a world of gratitude. I simply love her. And to Samuel, David and Ruth, may the good Lord bless you for your forbearances. Your games were cut short, the fun times were marginalized by reason of my call to duty. David shared the revelation he received from the Lord. That you will read in the last chapter. Samuel would always ask such inspiring questions; you would wonder at his wisdom. And Ruth revives my spirit, bringing tears to my eyes with her renditions in our local Church. My wife kept touch with the heavens in her prayers for me. Thanks so much. God bless you; may He keep us all faithful until the end.

In this second edition, Rev. Dr. Patrick Anyalewechi of Wilberforce University, Wilberforce Ohio played a major role in editing this book. His constructs and advise reengineered my thoughts and changed my concepts. It changed from a workbook to a story liner. Also Mrs Patience Nkechi Azuka added her wealth of experience towards this effort. To you all I owe so much for your time and counsel.

My friends in Malawi, Nigeria and South Africa have been partners in this work of discipleship and mentoring. They use our materials for training and coaching. I want to thank Bishop Emmanuel Mzumara of One Voice Malawi Church for the choice of coming under our leadership and having faith in what we do. Reverend and Pastor Mrs. Joseph and Patience Akazue of LIFA Christian Assembly in Sapele Nigeria have proved to be great ministry friends and partners. They pray earnestly for me. Thank you for your input in my life. Dr. Dan

Ozoko of Rural Evangelism Outreach, Nsukka Nigeria is another asset in this kingdom business. He pulls men and materials towards missions and rural evangelism. I salute your courage and tenacity. Dr. John and Carolyn Chukwu of Manchester England, have labored with me since 1982. I thank God for their simple, ongoing resolve to serve the Lord. Emmanuel and Udeme Ohia with Dr. Ferdinand Nweke are close partners who cannot be forgotten easily. Their work in Manchester England under Eternity Ministries has made impact in our time. Thank you for your labor in the house of faith. Ferdinand's books can set your heart on fire. You all refresh my spirit. May the Lord bless you and keep us until the day of His coming. Shalom!

Foreword

Jazzed & Inspired: My Story

I was appalled and fought for life as two persons struggled for a better grip of me. One was a monster, the other, an Angel. It was a matter of life and death amidst these two who laid claim to my life. They struggled and I cried for rescue, as I knew I was tearing apart; they were ready to 'yank' me into two. I despaired for breathe, gasping and breathing heavily. Suddenly I heard a voice: "Who will you serve?" Of course I needed a breath. I knew it was only God that could save at that time. So I yelled, "God", and immediately the hand of the monster (who I believe was the devil), fell off me. The angel led me up. We climbed stair ways which I did not see but knew we were climbing. At some point the devil continued to follow after us. I suddenly developed hatred towards him and some high degree of acceptance filled my heart towards the Angel. He, the Angel, told me not to be mindful of the devil; that he was a defeated foe. I was led to a golden gate but before then I had 'karatered' the devil on the chest and intended to fight (as was usual with my prior life). He fell and we gained a space by that. The gate open by itself, unmanned. And closed as soon as we got in but the devil who tried to rush in was locked out. The Angel asked me to sit down and take some rest. As he looked at me, he smiled. I woke up wondering what happened. This was May 14, 1982.

The next day I slept and found myself in a revolving universe, turning and churning. Everything and everyone was running for escape, running for fear and refuge. There was commotion. They said it was the end of all things. I was in this confusion and desired to escape but was locked in. It was obvious that I was doomed. Everything was in disarray; running away to nowhere. The sea was angry, swallowing and vomiting; mountains moved and collapsed on men and women as people sought refuge in them. The center could not hold anything. Nothing worked, everything was out of whack, dislodged and dismembered. I wondered why I was in this mess. I cried but did not hear any voice. It was late for me. As I cried, I woke up, confused, sweating, shaking to my bones. Really, there was no chance for me, but thanks goodness, it was a dream.

I kept these in my mind, wondering what experience I was having as I never knew the source of this information. The third night I went to bed again as I considered these developments. In the middle of the night, about 3am, a voice, so loud and clear spoke to my hearing. It was God speaking: "There is a way that seems right to a man, but the end of it is death." It was an unmistakable voice. The choice was clear and succinct. I was left to choose life or death. The next morning I told my uncle, Basil Okereke that I was going with him to Church. He had prayed ceaselessly for me. Surprised as he was, at the Grace of God Gospel Mission, Abakpa Nike, Enugu in Nigeria I walked up to the pastor after his sermon (uninvited) and asked him to pray for me for salvation. He did.

This new life has been a great wonder and experience. Since May 16, 1982 the experience and power, the glamour and peace, the knowledge and romance with the Holy Spirit is beyond scripting. As I grow I have suddenly discovered that my generation of believers and hub of those who have had a taste of glory are fast turning the leaf the other side. There seems to be a drought of grace in people, a delineation of a savory experience with the LOVE of their lives. The once forbidden fruit of the garden are eaten freely among the elect with no recourse to the dangers of hell. To be born again today is fashionable and stylish. Sin has been renamed, openly acceptable by both the clergy and the laity. The pew and pulpit stink with filth and the God of heaven is watching. As I write, I bear a heavy burden that would not let me surrender to frivolities and fleeting shows we call success. I will not yield to a new definition of Christianity that allows sin and luring signals of detestable behavior stifle life out of a remnant of the kingdom. I write to rekindle the fire that is put off in your soul. I write to ask you to revisit

Bethel and clean up the mess. I remember when Ezra and Nehemiah set to restore worship at Jerusalem; they appointed builders who laid the foundation of the temple of the Lord. The priests stood in their apparel with trumpets and the Levites with their cymbals to praise the Lord according to the ordinances of David. Scripture attests that as they sang and echoed responsively, the young men shouted 'glory, glory' because the foundation was laid. Because they saw some physical structure that never was by reason of the captivity in Babylon. But the old men wept. They wailed and groaned. There was confusion in the camp. Excitement and Weeping! Why? The old men recalled the glory they saw in the time of Solomon when the original temple was laid. They remembered their experience, the move of God, the revival that took place which would not even allow the priests to preach the word because the LORD appeared in the midst of His people. It was an experience that never faded away. You could cut through that glory. You could handle it and was not for show. (Ezra 3:8-13)

When you experience God and His glory, you'd understand what I mean. Moses had such an encounter; he would not proceed on the journey if God would not show him His glory (Exodus 33:12-23). At conversion, you had such a warm and explosive encounter with the Lord. May I ask, "What's going on now?" You need to revisit Bethel.

You need a personal revival. And that's what this piece of information in your hand is about. To get you back to your LOVER, Jesus Christ. To rekindle the fire that was put away by some weird wind. You must get fired up again. And that comes by way of personal discipleship.

Hey, listen to me, God me yanked into the kingdom; the Spirit got me jazzed with new wine. Today I can tell you it is sweet to serve Him, the lover of my soul. The times may have changed, strategies evolve and seasons offer new styles in our value delivery but God remains the same. Can you pick up your rusty Holy Script grand ma gave you at graduation and let's strike a deal. If you follow through the instructions of the Holy Bible and apply the gleaning from this manual alongside, you'd be fit, trimmed, trained and tamed for exploits as a disciple. He got me jazzed, filled me with His Spirit and inspired me to write to you NOW.

Chapter .1.

DISCLAIMER:
I Write For Dummies

Today's internet world and social media introduce us to how people follow an icon or a celebrity without a good knowledge about the person; or better still, without an intimate relationship with that person. They know about the person or are familiar with his or her comments or wisdom on social media and they just like this individual. That's great; anybody can do that. When it comes to discipleship, we are looking at a dedicated, planned out, disciplined life towards **knowing, involving** and **doing**. There is a set standard who is usually the Mentor or Teacher or Lord. This person is the target and arbitrator or somewhat "the big guy" everybody is answerable to or that holds the ace of the discipleship or mentoring program. His words are final, his methods are the outline for the process or scheme of things. In our situation, Jesus Christ is the Mentor.

I'd start by asking you to agree with my simple model of getting into the mainstream. My focus is to live life at its fullest in our community and nation at large. Beyond these locales, I have a home beyond the skies. It is a heavenly home where I intend to live forever with God. My occupation in heaven depends heavily on my engagement here in my local community or nation and specifically on how I steer my compass with other folks in my community. That is to say; how I live and operate with other people around me. So starting from home and my relationships within, I move to the streets and the community and affect my society. The way I navigate through this life-engaging drive determines the quality of the outcome of my 'living forever with God in heaven'. That sounds quite demanding, does it? But I know you can do it with me. This is how to get started:

ABC OF YOUR FAITH

A= Accept that you are a sinner and that only God, through His Son, Jesus Christ can help you out of the mess. Since we cannot help ourselves to overturn the power of sin, a higher power will and can help us out. This power is God. Accepting does not define you as a weakling but an intelligent decision to seek for help.

B= Believe in your heart that the Lord Jesus Christ has the power to save you from the rot and decay of human depravation and sin. Believe in His ability to clean you up from the inside with His blood which was spilled at Calvary. A trust today can earn you a confidence and access into His chambers. There you can ask for mercy.

C= Confess with your mouth, your sins, inabilities and human shortcomings. Ask for help. Confess Jesus as your Lord and Savior, tell your friends and relations that you got in love with a Man called Jesus. Go, tell your story.

The journey has just begun. You are now a child of God, a candidate of the kingdom of heaven. You will need some milk like a baby needs some colostrum at birth. Steadily we will get on this together and I must congratulate you for making a decision to join the train of heaven-bound Christians. Welcome on board. We will start our training by touching on the basics, fundamental issues and obligations.

In this chapter, we are going to discuss discipleship with particular reference to what builds or makes a disciple. The focus is "how can I become the disciple I am supposed to be?"

1. WHO IS A DISCIPLE?

The dictionary defines a disciple as a follower of a great teacher. It is derived from the verb meaning "to learn". The idea of discipleship is very old. It was common among the Greeks and a prominent feature of Judaism.

It always involved a Teacher-Student relationship. I Chronicle. 25:8; Isaiah 8:16. Common examples in the scriptures are: Moses and Joshua; Elijah and Elisha; Paul and Timothy; Jesus and the Apostles.

Discipleship is also a prominent and important concept in the New Testament. In Matthew 9: 14, Mark 2:18 we see the disciples of John the Baptist, in Matthew 22:15-17 we see the disciples of the Pharisees (Matthew 23:15).

Most often, however, the word 'disciple' was used to denote a relationship between Jesus and His followers. Luke 6:12-18; John 8:30, 31. We are going to streamline our study to being the disciples of Jesus Christ. In summary we say that a disciple is:
- ❖ A believer in Jesus Christ (Acts. 11:26)
- ❖ A learner in the School of Christ.

- ❖ One who is committed to a sacrificial life for His sake (Luke 14:26, 27 & 33)
- ❖ One who gets to fulfill or meet the obligations and requirements of discipleship; i.e. to replicate what the Lord has made of him, the disciple (Matthew 28:19)

2. THE DISCIPLE AND HIS MASTER

From previous discussions, we can see that there is a strong tie between the disciple and his master. The relationship is a Pupil - Master or Servant - Lord relationship. Jesus said, "The disciple is not above his master nor the servant above his Lord" Matthew 10:24,25. As a learner, the student has enrolled in the school and will finish his/her studies when he/she becomes like his Master. In Luke 6:40 it says " A pupil is not superior to his teacher, hut everyone when he is completely trained, readjusted, restored, set right and perfected, will be like his teacher" (Amplified). And this is what it means to he perfected in Christ Jesus Colossians 1:28.

DISCUSSIONS:

How do you see your relationship with Jesus Christ? What are your greatest aspirations (goals) as a Christian? Be very sincere.

To be like Christ (the Master), presented perfect in Christ, is all embracing. It involves being like Him in the following ways:

- ❖ Nature John 10:34-36; 1:12,13; 8:23; Colossians 3:1-5; 2 Peter 1:3-7
- ❖ Power and Strength Luke 10:1; John: 14:12; Acts. 1:8
- ❖ Life Style John 8:12; Matthew 5:14-16; 1 John 1:7
- ❖ Witnessing and Evangelism Mark I:15; John 17:18 (John 20:21)
- ❖ Facing Persecutions John 15:20; Mark 10:28-30
- ❖ Perseverance and Hope 1 Peter 2:21-24; Isaiah 53:1-11; Hebrew 10:35&36; Hebrew 12:1-5
- ❖ Focus and Determined Malachi 4:6; Luke 1:11; Matthew 11:2-14; Lamentations1:13-16

3. CALL TO DISCIPLESHIP

The call involves three things: Study: Matthew 11:20-28. Note: The law demands and metes out judgment; Grace and truth mediate and acquit the offender.

3.1 Coming: "Come unto me all ye" As many as come to me, I will in no wise cast out. Discipleship starts when one is born again i.e. coming to the

Master, Jesus Christ. There is no short cut to this. He said: "I am the way, the truth and the life, no one cometh to the Father except by me"

3.2 Learning of / from Him: Take my yoke upon you; let us be bonded together and accept my terms of leadership (discipleship) and learn of or from me. Learning is an integral part of discipleship. This involves hearing and speaking. To hear, one has to listen and what you hear depends on what you listen to. Jesus said, 'Learn from me ...'. The question here is: Who do you listen to and hence what are you hearing? The place of the word of God (the Bible) in your life is an indicator of who you are listening to and how much you are listening. A good student will respond to what he hears. One way is to verbalize his response. He can express appreciation or talk over with his teacher whatever is not understood. If you are a disciple, do you talk to your Master? How much dialogue do you have with Him? Your PRAYER LIFE indicates this. When last and how often do you really communicate with your master in prayer? Learning, for a disciple of Jesus Christ therefore, includes diligent study of the word of God and unceasing prayers, among other things.

3.3 Following: Following is both the proof and measure of the loyalty of the disciple to his master. Following is the application of all that the disciple has learned in total submission and humble obedience. Jesus said "If you know these things, happy are you if you do them. James puts it in another way "Do not fool yourself in just listening to His word, instead put it into practice" (James 1:22 Good News). Are you a doing disciple? Are you a practicing disciple? Are you a disciple who follows all the way? Only then can you ever dream of being like the Master.

Discussion
a) How did you come to personal relationship with Jesus Christ?
b) Share experiences of how you learn from Him.
c) What degree of following are you doing (Mention victories and pitfalls)?

4. CHARACTERISTICS OF A DISCIPLE
Take note: Romans 7:4-6... The law, motions of sin, your deliverance. The Natural man on parade: Ego; Selfish; Proud; Judgmental; Ease & Comfort; Materialism (exploiting for profit)
Solution: CRUCIFY THE FLESH (Galatians 5:24; Romans 8)

4.1 A Supreme love for the Master (Jesus Christ) = Affection; Love.
LOVE: seen from three perspectives from the original meaning; these are:

a) Eros, meaning the love that is rooted and culminates in sexual and lustful mindset and satisfaction.
b) Filial meaning the expression of ecstasy, and emotional affections
c) Agape meaning the affection and commitment to the other party without due process of acquaintance or foreknowledge of the person. It engages in sacrificial giving. It considers the other person first. It is to love one who does not deserve to be loved.

"If any man come to me and hate not his father, and mother and wife and children and brethren and sisters, yea and his own life also, he cannot he my disciple" (Luke 14:26). This does not mean that we should have animosity or ill-will in our hearts towards our relatives, but it does mean that our love for Christ should be so great that all other loves are secondary or even greatly diminished in comparison. Actually, the most difficult clause in the passage is the expression "...yea, and his own life also." Self love is one of the most stubborn hindrances to discipleship. Not until we willingly lay down our lives for Him are we in the position where we can be disciples indeed.

4.2 A Denial of Self – Sacrificial Living

This is the life that arises from an 'Agape' heart. A life that loves and gives; a life that loves sacrificially; thinks positively and is persistent while employing the tactic of persuasion in delivering the message; or carrying on with assigned duties by the Master. He simply loves his Master and wants to be like Him.

"If any man will come after me, let him deny himself..." (Matthew 16:24). Denial of self is not the same as self denial. The later means forgoing certain foods, pleasures or possessions. But denial of self means such complete submission to the Lordship of Christ that self has no rights or authority at all. It means that self abdicates (gives up its legal rights and worth) the throne.

4.3 A Deliberate Choosing of the Cross = Commitment

Consider 1Peter 2:21; Galatians 6:14-17. Paul wrote: From henceforth, let no man trouble me, for I bear on my body the mark of our Lord Jesus Christ. There is a mark which all disciples bear. It is called the mark of Christ. It is associated with the CROSS. The cross is not a milk shake from McDonalds, neither is it a certain comfort and ease that we claim and possess for selfish ends. "If any man will come after me, let him deny himself and take up his cross..." (Matthew 16:24). The cross is not some physical infirmity or mental anguish; these things are common to all men. The cross is a pathway of suffering that is deliberately chosen. It is a path, which, so far as this world goes, is one of dishonor and reproach. The cross symbolizes the shame, persecution and abuse which the world heaped upon the Son of God and which it will heap on all who choose to stand against its trend. Any believer can avoid the cross simply by being conformed to the world, and its ways, but the disciple will not. The commitment to bear the cross to your Golgotha is contingent on the disciple. Suffice to say that this disciple is a slave both to the Lord and to the world. Before the proclamation that freed slaves in the USA, bond slaves were branded by their owners with hot iron on their backs. The Holy Spirit has branded you for Christ.

Types of Cross:
These include racial discrimination; prejudice and unjust treatment at work place; denial of rights of equality; voluntary denying oneself of lunch so that money saved can be sent to mission fields; trek to witness the gospel to people; working extra hours and use money realized from this to help the poor.

4.4 A Life Spent in Following Christ = Submit, Obey & Walk (SOW principle)
The SOW principle bears on the spiritual, financial and physical well-being of the disciple. The law of multiplication is a universal one that anyone

can assess and be blessed by God. Whatever a man sows that he shall also reap (Galatians 6:7).

"If any man will come after me, let him deny himself and take up his cross and follow me" (Matthew 16:24). To understand what this means, one ought to ask oneself, 'what characterized the life of the Lord Jesus?' It was a life of obedience to the will of God. It was a life lived in the power of the Holy Spirit. It was a life of unselfish service for others. It was a life of patience and long suffering in the face of the gravest wrongs or mistreatments. It was a life of kindness, of faithfulness and of devotion. (Galatians 5:22&23). In order to be like his Master, he must walk as He walked. (Philippians 2:5-11). We must exhibit fruits of Christ-likeness (John 15:8).

4.5 A Fervent love for All who Belong to Christ = Serving Others

"By this shall all men know that ye are my disciples, if ye have love one to another" (John 13:35). This is the love that esteems others better than oneself. It is the love that covers a multitude of sins; a love that is characterized by I Corinthians 13: 4-7. It is not sensual, not filial but agape kind of love. Compare John 3:16 with 1 John 3:16. Without this love, discipleship would be a cold, legalistic asceticism (one who does not allow himself bodily pleasures for religious reasons; call him a fanatic).

4.6 An Unswerving Continuance in His Word = Knowing and Doing the WORD

"If ye continue in my word, then are ye my disciples indeed" John 8:31. For real discipleship, there should be continuance in the study of the word of God. It is easy enough to start well, to burst forth in a blaze of glory and ecstasy but the test of reality is the endurance to the end. Any man who looks back after putting his hand to the plough is not fit for the kingdom of God. (Luke 9:62). Spasmodic (irregular) obedience to the scriptures will not be enough to sustain a Christian for the present times we are in. Christ wants those who will follow Him in continuous, constant, unquestioning obedience (Hebrews 10:38).

4.7 A Forsaking of ALL To follow Him = Resignation

Jim Elliot, a missionary to Ecuador said: "He is no fool who gives up what he cannot keep to get what he cannot have". This is following, obeying and serving. It is likened to losing all self worth and specs of importance you ascribe to yourself and throwing in the towel, most of the times, being 'stupid' if you may; then with one ascent and unbending resolve, journey with the Master.

"So likewise, whosoever he be of you that forsakes not all that he hath, he cannot be my disciple" Luke 14:33. What is meant by forsaking

ALL? It means a handing over of all one's possessions to the Master for disbursements. The man who forsakes himself and all possessions does not become a loafer or a wanderer but he works hard to provide for his current needs of his family and himself. Since the passion of his life is to advance the course of Christ, he invests everything above current needs in the work of the Lord and leaves the future with God. In seeking first the kingdom of God and His righteousness, he believes that he will never lack anything. He does not expect to spend all his life accumulating riches and wealth he will leave one day (or that will disappear and leave him a destitute to his own dismay). He wants to obey the Lord's injunctions against laying up treasures on earth while lending himself as an instrument of honor to his family, the Church and his community according to the multitude of God's grace and provisioning.

Take a practical step, try reading and practicing the book "In His Steps" by Charles Sheldon. There is nothing as real and satisfying as following and doing the exact procedures as laid down by the Lord Jesus Christ.

NOTES:

The clause "If any man", "If ye", "whosoever" are very important. They mean that the onus is on the individual. In other words, the presence or lack of these characteristics depends on the individual.

Chapter 2.

FAITH:
Nuggets For The New Life

The new birth experience comes on the heels of a belief or trust you have in the Lord to save you from sin. You saw it operationally active and evident by the 'taste' and passion you are experiencing. The 'taste' is the different desire for righteousness, a taste for something eternally fulfilling and a refrain from what is socially and morally debasing. You just noticed there is a hunger for reality; some search engine grows up within your heart to search for God and do His will. There is a growing desire to know Him. Faith, by orthodox definition, is the substance of things hoped for, evidence of things not seen. It is a handle on what we cannot see.

It seems to me that faith is a fundamental tool kit we need to access God's resources or even approach Him. Jesus said to His followers, 'have faith in God' and it conveys a necessity to hold on to the word of God at all times, in all circumstances. The nugget of Faith is as important in following our Lord as the air we breathe to sustain life. No wonder the writer of Hebrews goes on to say that with faith, our ancestors in the race to heaven secured a good report and were not cast away. Believing the word for what it says and assures; taking the word of promise as written and acting on the revealed Rhema is what you need to live by. In everything, believe God for what He says about you, about your future and about your destiny. This is sufficient for life and ministry.

To believe is to wholly accept His terms and go all the way according to His instructions and directions. In the world we prove things, we analyze probabilities (sometimes get into over analysis to the extent of committing 'analysis paralysis'), we go for what the eye can see, what the mouth can taste and what our feelings are. Because the natural man is short sighted, unable to see the spiritual, he is limited to programs that surround the cosmos. To walk with God, we must have a simple, child-like trust that God is, and willing to save, to transform, and change our lives. The transformation is God-based, the foundation of the change unshaken. Faith is a personal trust in Jesus Christ (Romans 4, 5:23-25; 5:1).

In prayer, faith is the confidence we have in Him that if we ask anything according to His will, He will hear us and answer (1 John 5:14-15). As used in reference to unseen things; faith gives substance to those things unseen so that we act upon the conviction of their reality (Hebrews 11:1-3).As a charge to man, faith is a command for man to unmask self of the 'ability' and 'skills' he is so engrossed with, that it becomes a tool for success in life. He is to hands-off everything and leave them with God's monitoring and supervision; Jesus told the disciples: "Have faith in God" Mark 11:22&23.

Faith is the substance of things not seen, the evidence of things hoped for. But without faith it is impossible to please Him for he who comes to God must believe that He is and that He is the rewarder of those who diligently seek Him. Hebrews 11:1&6.

Faith is taking or trusting God for His word and behaving in consonance with that word. It is ignoring or putting away from our minds, psyches and thoughts, the false doctrine of men that come from philosophy, traditions, cultures and religions.

These come to us through the news media, friends, relations by our constant associations and dealings with them. Faith therefore is believing God's word and trashing these others and sustaining our spirits with what God says about us, about our worlds and about the circumstances around us. Faith is the substance of things hoped for, the evidence of things not seen.

FAITH IS NOT...

1. Absence of fear of the unknown. Faith is having the fear of God, watching in awe and being engulfed in a "wait time" to see God unfold events. Example is Noah, Abraham, Sarah, etc. Genesis 6 through 9: 17; Hebrews 11:7
2. Faith is not having the answer or results of your engagement as you want it. The vision beclouds what is in the physical; results may delay but faith persists (the end here justifies the means). Genesis 12:1-9; 17:1-8; Hebrews 11:8-19
3. It is not an eradication or absence of the five senses (sight, taste, touch/feeling, smell, hearing) but superimposed effect on their limitations and a stretch of what the five senses cannot do.
4. It is not a rhetoric expression or a religious feeling. It is an indulgence.
5. Faith is not result-driven on the cosmos (here the end does not justify the means) but rather, it distils in

an outcome akin to heaven's measure and validations such as faithfulness; receiving the crown, being accepted into God's bosom. Result is not measured by physical output on Earth only but a total package and overall productivity index which only God appoints. It is the currency with which you transact business with God.

6. Faith is not the absence of pain or pressure; it is not also the absence of joy. Pain and pressure may be experienced as a result of having faith and engaging in faithful service in the work. God may decide to keep silent and watch events unfold. This may be because He intends to sharpen the disciple or make him more like Jesus by the things he is suffering. But watch, the disciple comes out better, refined, more mature and able to represent God better.

7. Faith is not the ability to make wealth or a sudden emergence of fortune that classifies the poor as a faithless bunch. It is a confidence in God that assures a believer that even in the face of want and scarcity, God remains the focal point of life.

Let us consider some levels of Faith:
1. The Faith that believes and introduces us into the presence of the Father. God first calls us to Himself. As the Holy Spirit ploughs and prepares our hearts, the word is planted and as God stretches out His hand to us, introducing Jesus Christ, His Son, we yield to this invitation. Imagine a baby, walking along

the way suddenly comes face to face with a mad, furious wolf. Helpless, determined to survive starts running along the road that leads to nowhere. The wolf is racing after him and suddenly this hunter appears, fully loaded with ammunitions in his automatic weapon. The hunter stretches out his arm and the baby is safe. It will be foolishness to refuse such an offer. That is what God (the hunter) is to man (the baby) in the face of Satan (the wolf). This is the level of faith that believes in the hunter for salvation.
2. The Faith that receives. You know the good things of life: good health, money, anointing, new jobs and promotions; open business opportunities; marriage between a man and a wife; academic successes, etc.
3. The Faith that gives. This is the level of spending for your faith; having a vision from God that propels you to invest in the kingdom with the hope that God is in partnership with you in the kingdom business you have enlisted in.
4. The Faith that spends and is ready to be spent. Propelled by the vision (grace of the Lord), he has a mission to accomplish, he spends his life in serving others as an offering (completely poured out like a drink offering) for the course of Christ. You spend your life and resources and you are spent from inside out. Everything about you is poured out like a libation to the Lord, His work and His people. To the world, you look stupid and un-counseled. It's all

because you see a glory that others are not seeing. You are propelled by the end of the vision; by heaven and the King of the kingdom before you.

5. The Faith that dies. He says 'If perish, I perish'. This fellow is dead to the flesh and has lost his self-esteem, pride and worldly appeal to life. His grip on material things is loose and relaxed, ready to let go and use it for the gospel. This comes from the cue of the vision of heaven and the Lord's appearing. John 12:24-26 (the seed must die; the way up is always down), Romans 12:1-3 (Living sacrifices; you kill it before offering it as a sacrifice) 2 Timothy 4:6-8: we see a demand from God for our lives to be poured out for His work.

With eyes on heaven, undaunted by events in the world, they have a vision, are consumed by the glory that goes with it, they push on to the saving of their souls. They embrace the promise and confessed that they are strangers and pilgrims on Earth. They are not mindful of the country they came out of otherwise they would have reason to go back, instead, they look for a better city whose maker and builder is God. This is Faith.

OPERATING FAITH

There can be no true discipleship without a profound faith in the living God. He who would do exploits for the Lord must first trust Him implicitly. The discussion here is going to center on the disciple's confidence in His Master in the light of the cost of his venture: discipleship. The deliberate choosing of the cross to follow the Lord has its "associated consequences" and "disgusting experiences." But faith in the Master would renew and refresh the aching soul; reminding him that after all, there is a great eternal dividend underlying his choice of the cross and the journey towards heavenly glories.

The disciple must live by faith. It is faith when self is abdicated, thus denied; faith when there is sorrow and anguish along Golgotha's pathway; faith when in loving ALL who are the same fold, there may be some form of abuse and misunderstanding; sometime, a casting away and a rejection. In deciding to go all the way with the Master, some form of self-pity, a feel of empathy (especially in the midst of aggravated assaults from within the body of Christ... tribal maligning; ethnic maundering; and social economic enslavement) may overcome the disciple and thus such a one begins to consider a recourse to the old ways of living. At such times, may you hear the voice of the Spirit saying 'we are not of them that draw back unto perdition, but are of they that forge on to the saving of the soul... for if any man draws back, my soul will not have pleasure in him"

"But without faith it is impossible to please and be satisfactory to Him. For whoever would come to God must necessarily believe that God exists and that He is the rewarder of those who earnestly and diligently seek HIM out" (Hebrews 11:6 Amplified).

Faith, it must be understood, is synonymous with trust, confidence and reliance on God to do the supernatural especially in the dark tunnel of hopelessness. We see men of old display such faith even when their salvation was not in sight.

Abraham: Called to leave his country and kinsmen (Genesis 12:1); Separated from Lot (Genesis 13:9); Asked to offer Isaac, his only son (Genesis 22: 1-3).
Noah: To build an ark; Preached about the end-time as he engaged in the construction of the ark for 120 years.
Moses: Left the kingship position due him and went into wilderness to sojourn with animals. He esteemed the reproach of Christ (of the people of God) greater riches than the treasures in Egypt (of sin).

The scriptures attest to many who, because of their consecration and dedication to follow the Lord, gave up their lives and properties to see that they were faithful to the end. (Hebrews 11:33-40)

THOUGHT:

If you are to experience the things those men and women of old encountered, would you still follow and learn of and from the Master?
Would you continue as a disciple?

Assignment:
Name some problems associated with having an unflinching faith at desperate moments. Differentiate between the faith to receive miracles and the faith to give and if possible, die for the course of the gospel. When pressures and challenges of life take center stage, what options are available as escape routes if one must remain a disciple?

ASSURANCE OF SALVATION

"Therefore, since we have been made right in God's sight by faith, we have peace with God because of what Jesus Christ our Lord has done for us. Through whom we have access by faith into this grace in which we stand; and we rejoice in the hope of the glory of God" Romans 5:1&2

When you buy a car, the Department of Motor Vehicles' license office insists that you insure your car against incidental damage or collision. The same goes with a purchase of your home. Your home insurance is a condition to the purchase you make. The government demands that we insure these assets in the event the unexpected happens. An insurance company underwrites accruable expenses. Have you ever asked this question: What if the insurance company goes under water? Who pays? Who comes to the rescue? Banks and insurance companies are usually insured under a "big brother." These are NDIC or reinsurance companies; an example is American International Group, Inc. (AIG). AIG is an American multinational insurance corporation with more than 88 million customers in 130 countries. AIG companies employ over 64,000 people in ninety countries. The company operates through three core businesses: AIG Property Casualty, AIG Life and Retirement, and United Guaranty Corporation (UGC). AIG Property Casualty provides insurance products for commercial, institutional, and individual customers. AIG Life and Retirement provides life insurance and retirement services in the United States, and UGC focus on mortgage guaranty insurance and mortgage insurance. AIG also focuses on global capital markets operations, direct investment, and retained interests. Now you understand why the Fed swiftly bailed the AIG when it threatened to pull the plug on the financial market. As AIG provides cover to the insurance companies, insurance companies provide the same cover to the man on the street. The assurance (peace of mind) the consumer has is resting on the fact that should the worst happen, AIG or NDIC will come to the rescue.

By faith, we walk with the Lord, and while the journey of life lasts, we have access to education, or whatever lends to success in life. Sometimes, our faith rests on the bottom line. The assurance we have is in the fact that after all things are completed, we have this confidence that Jesus Christ will definitely bail us out of the mire, just because we have faith in Him. The promise of the Father "to give us the kingdom" is an established line of truth and a promissory note that we can cash any time because, by the Holy Ghost, it has been engraved in our hearts forever and affirmed by the word of God.

At conversion, God made an exchange. He removed the heart of stone and replaced it with the heart of flesh. We became born again and our names were written in the Book of Life. The Holy Spirit came in and took charge, and we were changed. The presence of the Holy Spirit is the receipt for the transaction, and the peace oozing out of such transformation is proof that there is an occupant in the house that God just acquired. This is assurance of salvation. 1 John 5:11-13; John 1:12; Romans 10:9; John 10:28&29.

If we confess our sins, He is faithful and just to forgive us our sins and to cleanse us from all unrighteousness. What, then, can separate us from the love of God, which is in Christ Jesus?

From Romans chapter five and your personal experience, an unforgettable change took place in your life. You become a true believer, no matter where life had taken you to. Now you are being justified by faith, you have peace with God. Knowing that the holy, righteous God cannot be at peace with a sinner under the guilt or burden of sin, you have been made righteous on the ticket of our Lord Jesus

Christ. You are justified, made to stand right and straight before God. This justification takes away the guilt, and so makes way for peace in your heart. This is through our Lord Jesus Christ.

As Matthew Henry points out: "The saints" happy state is a state of grace. Into this grace we are brought, which teaches that we were not born in this state. We could not have got into it of ourselves, but we are led into it, as pardoned offenders. Therein we stand, a posture that denotes perseverance; we stand firm and safe, upheld by the power of God."

And those who have hope for the glory of God hereafter, have enough to rejoice in now. Tribulation worketh patience, not in and of itself, but the powerful grace of God working in and with the tribulation. Patient sufferers have most of the Divine consolations, which abound as afflictions abound. It works needful experience of ourselves. This hope will not disappoint, because it is sealed with the Holy Spirit as a Spirit of love. It is the gracious work of the blessed Spirit to shed abroad the love of God in the hearts of all the saints. A right sense of God's love to us, will make us not ashamed, either of our hope, or of our sufferings for him. "And through Him to reconcile to Himself all things, whether things on earth or things in heaven, by making peace through the blood of His cross." Colossians 1:20

Christ in his human nature is the visible discovery of the invisible God, and he that hath seen

Him hath seen the Father. Let us adore these mysteries in humble faith, and behold the glory of the Lord in Christ Jesus. He was born or begotten before all the creation, before any creature was made; which is the Scripture way of representing eternity, and by which the eternity of God is represented to us. All things being created by Him, were created for him; being made by his power, they were made according to his pleasure, and for his praise and glory. He not only created them all at first, but it is by the word of his power that they are upheld. Christ as Mediator is the Head of the body, the church; all grace and strength are from him; and the church is his body. All fullness dwells in him; a fullness of merit and righteousness, of strength and grace for us. God showed his justice in requiring full satisfaction. This mode of redeeming mankind by the death of Christ was most suitable.

Here is presented to our view the method of being reconciled. And that, notwithstanding the hatred of sin on God's part, it pleased God to reconcile fallen man to himself. If convinced that we were enemies in our minds by wicked works, and that we are now reconciled to God by the sacrifice and death of Christ in our nature, we shall not attempt to explain away, nor yet think fully to comprehend these mysteries; but we shall see the glory of this plan of redemption, and rejoice in the hope set before us. If this be so, that God's love is so great to us, what shall we do now for God? Be frequent in prayer, and abound in holy duties; and live no more to yourselves, but to Christ. Christ died for us. But wherefore? That we should still live in sin? No; but that we should die to sin, and live henceforth not to ourselves, but to Him.

GRACE, MERCY & TRUTH

In my book, "Digging for Gold" I wrote some fine lines regarding this subject. Here's an excerpt: Suppose Osama bin Laden and all the people who masterminded the 9/11 attack on the World Trade Center had been in the United States before September 2011, and there was rumor that foreign faces were seen around the Capitol and Pentagon. Suddenly, the terrorists hit. New York firefighters gave their lives trying to rescue people trapped in the World Trade Center. Suppose the only ones trapped were the terrorists who caused the explosion.

Suppose it was Osama bin Laden who was stuck in that building, and he was known to have masterminded the crime. Make it more personal: imagine a soldier who lost his wife and child in the World Trade Center because Osama bin Laden ordered those suicide bombings. Imagine him carrying Osama bin Laden out of the smoke and dust, giving him water, and nursing him back to health. Unthinkable! Isn't it? That's getting closer to grace.

Defining Truth

Truth is a validated and proven fact of life. It has no gray area of interpretation but stands out with a perfect conclusion of an issue, statement or analysis in any given environment or within a group. Truth is a constant, and constants do not change. They are absolutes, never shifting from their positions. Truth is a personality that has potential to grow and blossom. Truth is rooted in the eternal God who is all powerful and unchangeable. Therefore, His promises cannot fail.

Jesus prayed, "Sanctify them by the truth; Your word is Truth" (John 17:17). Not only can we depend on Scripture, but we can be transformed and sanctified by it.

What Truth Is Not

Truth does not change with changing circumstances, though it is an agent of change. Truth is not a moral guide. Jesus declared, "I am the way, the truth and the life; no man comes to the Father but by Me" (John 14:6). He did not say He would show the truth or teach the truth or model the truth. He is the truth. He is truth personified. He is the source of all truth, the embodiment of truth and therefore, the reference point for evaluating all truth claims. Truth is not a suggestion to live right or do some spectacular things. Truth does not advertise itself but stays docile and calm, affecting its hearers.

Truth is not an idea or a localized or regionalized code of behavior; it outlives the carrier.

Name other things that truth is not:
Truth is seen as a vapor that spreads, never contained or restricted. Share your insights into the nature and constitution of this vapor.

What Truth Is:
1. Truth is life.
2. Truth changes lives and sanctifies the heart
3. Truth, when used to describe people, can show integrity of thoughts, speech, or actions. Truth is the bedrock of human relationships (Exodus 20:16).
4. Truth is reality. It's the way things really are. In over 50 percent of Paul's writings in John, the New Testament uses "truth" (aletheia in Greek, meaning "disclosure").
5. To know the truth is to see accurately. To believe what is not true is to be blind. God has written His truth on human hearts, in the conscience (Romans 2:15). When the world hears truth, if spoken graciously, many are drawn to it by the moral vacuum they feel. The heart longs for truth; even the heart that rejects it.
6. The Holy Spirit leads men into truth (John 16:13). Christ's disciples know the truth (John 8:32), they do the truth (John 3:21), and they abide in the truth (John 8:44). We are commanded to know the truth

(1 Timothy 4:3), handle the truth accurately (2 Timothy 2:25), and avoid doctrinal untruths (2 Timothy 2:18). The "belt of truth" holds together our spiritual armor (Ephesians 6:14).
7. Jesus is the truth and the life.

Lies the Devil Is Passing On in Our Age and Churches
1. "Open theology," which contends that God doesn't know what future choices people will make
2. Waning belief in an eternal punishment or human depravity. It is proposed that hell fire is what you experience on earth, whatever your situation dictates; belief that a good God cannot put people in hell, so there is no hell.
3. Sexual behavior is acceptable, even outside of marriage. "We are bed mates; nothing is wrong with it."
4. Heterosexuals and homosexuals are the same. Lesbians and gays should be given equal opportunity to lead the church. It is politically acceptable. (Permit me to say, "Even my dog would oppose that and groan at the church")
5. The Scripture is not the authoritative source for living. "I will not allow God's Word to persuade me to believe what I do not like; what is contrary to what I have always believed and want to believe." The question should be asked, "Do I believe it's correct when it offends me?"

6. Open-ended theology: a "you can have it all" worldview is a hodgepodge of biblical truth, undefined spirituality, and psychology, with twelve-step recovery and self-affirmations. The open-ended theology is a church-free build-it-yourself spirituality that never condemns. It speaks often of a higher power—sometimes God, sometimes Jesus.

7. Generic spirituality: all roads lead to heaven. Karma. Mohammed. Reincarnation. Buddhism. Hinduism. New Age. Angel-guided living. It's a "Have it your way" designer religion made to order for a post-Christian culture. "Now the Bereans were of more noble character than the Thessalonians, for they received the message with great eagerness and examined the Scriptures every day to see if what Paul said was true" (Acts 17:11).

8. Amorphous, shape-shifting faith that slides to the contours of individual preferences. This nurtures our tendency to self-edification, in which we strive to be our own gods, setting our own standards, and controlling our own mini-universes. "Do it my way" kind of thing.

9. Hydra-headed path to God, which suggests that "the biggest mistakes humans make is to believe there is only one way." And adds that there are many diverse paths leading to what you call God. In the meantime, God says, "Neither is there any other name under heaven given among men whereby we must be saved" (Acts 4:12). Jesus remains the hub

and center of all creation and path to God. There is no alternative path to seeking God.

10. "Truth is whatever you sincerely believe is true." "There's no such thing as truth"—is this a true statement? If so, then the statement proves itself wrong. (Why does anyone go to college to learn truth from professors who believe there is no truth?) Jesus Christ is the truth and the life.

11. Moral relativism: church pews filled with all-inclusive doctrinal backlashes, "come as you are; remain the way you came"; "gather the tithes and offerings for our next project." This has no spiritual content toward heaven or toward God. Moral relativism has no underlying substance to hold its structure or contend for what it believes is right. Relativism floats on the whims of what is socially and all-inclusively prevailing. It has no core values.

12. Freedom to live in sin because we are "saved by grace, do anything under grace (including living in sin), and still are on our way to heaven." A woman preacher (a televangelist) walked away from her marriage without biblical grounds because, in her words, "The Holy Spirit gave me peace about it." She also said, "It is turning out for the glory of God, and the ministry is moving forward." She is still preaching and raising followers in the church, claiming the spiritual high ground. She said, "I've never been so close to God." There is a looming "Ichabod" on the wall!

FREE FROM SIN

It is an exciting experience to fall in love. You remember your first lover? In this instance, Jesus Christ, the lover of your soul comes to stage. God loved you while you were still in sin. And arising from the fact that you had no bargain in this, Jesus paid a full ransom for your sins and bought you back, though you had strayed away from God. Today, you are free from sin as a result of His blood that was used to atone (make a repudiation for you). This same blood is used to make a defense for your protection and security. Again, you are free from the power of sin since the power of evil has been broken in your system and presently, there is a free flow of the power of God inside of you. The Lord declares:

"For sin shall not have dominion over you." This brings us to the nugget of indwelling power of the Holy Spirit, brought about by the new birth. The shift from old ways of living implies a complete cascading from the lifestyle of sin. There is a detour into a new lifestyle of righteousness and not to continue in the old ways of doing business. This means a complete departure from traditions of men, culturally induced thinking and the world's suggestions and practices. The indwelling power of God (in another phrase, called the Holy Spirit) or the seed of God is planted in your heart. By this implant you have a new nature of God. You are a son of God. This incorruptible seed begins a work that makes you thirst after the righteousness of God. It says 'no' to sin and the appeals of the world systems.

There is then no taste or desire for anything ungodly. As you post this emblem in your character, your friends may call you names and brand you a 'fanatic'. In the social media, your comments are different, your postings point to the type of seed in you. You are different from other guys. You are a child of God.

YOU ARE IN LOVE

Jesus, the passionate lover of our souls has this to say: "Thou shalt love the Lord thy God with all thy heart, and with all thy soul, and with all thy mind. This is the first and great commandment. And the second is like unto it, Thou shalt love thy neighbor as thyself. On these two commandments hang all the law and the prophets." Matthew 22:37-40 (KJV)

As I have loved you, so you likewise love one another and by so doing, you fulfill the law and the prophets. By implication Jesus is telling us to engage in the act of love towards humanity and God. When we consider all His acts of kindness and mercy, the selfless sacrifice on the cross and His daily supplies, we owe Him an obligation to simply love the Father and the Son (not excluding the Spirit) in return. He says, "love the Lord thy God with all thy heart." I have discovered that if I can maintain my gaze at the cross, at Jesus Christ and recollect all that happened there, I will always be poised to maintain a good relationship with Him. This relationship keeps me from doing anything contrary to my Lover's concerns and care-about. My love for Him provides a confidence that He will attend to my needs and keep me from evil. As I think about God's love, I am indebted to His service and as long as this relationship stands secured and valid, I can do anything for Him. I am in love, remember! The same story you can tell too.

This same love story makes a man spend anything for his lover; the lovers get to talk and stay together. They do things in common. And so in the secret place of their room, there they spend hours relating and talking and listening to each other. This we enjoy in the place of prayer and answers. Love stories around your new birth need to be rekindled. You are in a free fall of love. Because this love of Christ is so consuming and deep, it cannot be understood by those outside this terrain, the reason why your friends are confused at your commitment to it. Let the love of God be shed broadly in your heart because He first loved us (even while we were yet sinners, the righteous loving the unrighteous, Christ Jesus died for us).

Chapter .3.

THE PLAY AND THE PRACTICE

Disciples are made, not born. This is by training. Luke 6:40 says, "The disciple is not superior to his teacher, the fully trained disciple will always be like his teacher" (Jerusalem Bible) Training can be formal or informal, external or/and personal. Below, though not comprehensive, are ways by which the individual can build up himself in a personal discipleship—without which the aspirations to ever be like the Master will be a mirage.

1. START WITH A ROMANTIC CONVERSATION

Romantic conversation between two lovers can be deep. Two lovers can spend hours with each other without looking at the passage of time. This is same with prayer; a communication dialogue with you and your lover, Jesus Christ. Prayer is a communication with the heavenly Father through the access of the Lord Jesus Christ, using the power and strength of the Holy Spirit. It is the soul of man talking to God. It is not optional because men ought always to pray. Real prayer is life creating and life changing because it is God-touching. The closer we come to the heartbeat of God, the more we see our need and desire to conform to Christ.

The world being a global village of sort, information is on the palm or on every mobile device. The ability to digest and retain these information provide tools to go to 'war' with. Since Scripture says we should pray without ceasing, the array of data and information system and connectivity with the Spirit ought to prompt us to engage in spiritual warfare. Prayers that touch the heavens can be muted and praying in the Holy Ghost can be effectual even under closed doors. The burden of unfolding events in the world of politics and emergence of anti-Christ policies call for concern. Believers can use Go-to-meeting software or Skype conferencing tool to communicate during prayer meetings at different locations. If the millions of gamma rays in an electronic emission cannot be measured, then the force of prayers would not be withstood by any force.

As disciples who will follow where the Master leads, we need to take the steps of our Master in prayer. Christ was a man of prayer. He rose up early before day and went to a lonely place and there He prayed. Today, He lives to make intercessions for us (Mark 1:35; Hebrews 7:25). Given the demands of the over-crowded activities of the day and the surge of information flowing through our devices, disciples ought to create time for the important things of life, among which prayer occupies a big space. For example, you can set alarm on your phone and get up in the night while folks are sleeping, to pray.

Prayer should be an activity to be enjoyed. If you fix your heart on what is good and lovely, you'd always have reason to worship or to give thanks for the good things and people in your life. Keep it positive and be happy with the abundance God has blessed you with. Take a look at your environment and you will discover that your situation is not, after all, the worst of its kind. Be grateful for life, be grateful for your salvation and soon you would burst out with singing and worshipping. Count your blessings, name them one after the other and you will be amazed at what God has done for you. Sometimes you are overwhelmed by the demands of the day. At such moment, just sit back and think on His goodness and mercies. Be expressive when you pray. Talk to God as if you are talking to a friend. He is right where you are. Be yourself and communicate freely. Wait to get a feed back. You must not hurry out of that spot. Wait, He speaks to His children.

2. THE WORD WORKS WONDERS (WWW)

The word of God in you defines you, directs your doctrine and forms the basis of your prayer life. The word of life models our lifestyle and shapes the way we do things. No wonder the Scripture tell us in 2 Timothy 2:15: "Study to show yourself approved unto God, a work man that need not be ashamed; rightly dividing the word of truth"; and Jesus told His disciples, "Search the scriptures for in them you think you have eternal life and they are they which testify of me" John 5:39. To grasp the juice from the Scriptures, the word of God must be read, studied, meditated on, memorized and practiced. Before we can be adequately equipped to confront the devil, we must spend time with the word of God (66 Books of the Bible). As a new Christian you can start with such books as Gospel of John, the Synoptic Gospels, Psalm, Proverbs etc.

But to put the study of the word in the right perspective and capture the cream of the books, we must strategically and systematically give serious attention to the discovery of truth. Take an example when you dated your wife; life was great and for every moment, you read her mail. She posted something to you. Text messages filled your phone and everything could wait just for you to read her mail or text. On her part, the lady did not sleep, she spent hours late in the night, cuddling her pillows, waiting for the day of her wedding. Love and affection drove both of you. You could not do anything without each other. The same goes with you and the Son, Jesus Christ. He is the love of your life and wants to relate with you. I discover the only way to know Him deeply is to read His love letter or mail to you. This letter is the Holy Bible. The Bible has a complete narrative about the Father, the Son and his Holy Spirit. The more of the word in you, the more the friendship, the passion and intimacy you develop with Him. All other appeals will fade away if you keep a close, frequent touch with Him through His word. Here is a simple way to do it:

a. Book Study (chapter by chapter); taking the books individually to study the theme, dates, archaeology and main idea of the writing, characters involved, lessons learned, and sins/pitfalls to avoid. E.g. Book of Philemon.

b. Character Study (Personality Study); we choose a character to find out all about the person: his/her background, parentage, nativity, faith, struggles, exploits, and contributions to Jewish or Christian community. Did he/she run the race to the end; if not, why. E.g. The life of Moses

c. Topical Study (Subject Study); choose a topic from among the various doctrines of the Christian faith, take for example "Second Coming of Jesus Christ." This type of study takes one through many books of the Bible and the student tries to compare scripture with scripture to bring out a balanced thought and logical truth.

d. Comparative/ Analytical Study; taking two or more scenarios (cultures, geography, settlements, trades and occupations of a people) to discover the basis for writing and understand underlying beliefs and ways of living of the people of old; then employing same to the present day challenges of the Christian faith and living. You must use good commentaries, Bible dictionaries, and history books.

By just Reading the Bible, you are obtaining information and gaining general knowledge about a subject. (Revelations 1:3). Reading provides the Logos and makes the written word bare and accessible. During Meditation; you are thinking over the word that was heard or read with a view to a regenerated mind. Philippians 4:8; Romans 12:1. The practice of meditation on the word of God is best done during the Quiet Time or your devotional moment. It is a time to chew the cord (as we find in ruminants with 4 chambered stomachs); to ponder over what was said in the church or studied in a house fellowship. Most often this is the time the Rhema of the Word is received. Rhema is the revealed, spirit-powered word that changes lives. The Holy Spirit reveals the Rhema. Studying involves a diligent search for truth. It takes time and effort and more important, the uses of resources such as concordance, dictionaries, and commentaries, study Bibles are applied here. Memorizing the Bible is taking into memory, Bible passages and verses for use at unscheduled, prompt times. Doing the Word is the art and act of living the word and obeying its instructions and commands. In studying, reading, meditation and memorizing the word will be effort in futility if nothing is done about it in daily living. Like Ezra, he purposed in his heart, to do, read and teach others same words among his king's men. (Ezra 7:10) The quality and quantity of the word of God in you determines how far you can go in your walk with the Master. It feeds your faith. In fact it is the foundation on which every other thing is built.

3. YOU CAN GO WITHOUT FOOD

The man of God was unperturbed, preaching with vibrancy and force. His words thundered into the heavens with every punch at sin. The Spirits came to town with the introduction of a new song he just formed and it was an electrifying meeting. The Church went wild because the Spirit came with gifting and healing. All was not as planned; the Holy Ghost had taken over the service at this time. It was God's business. Everybody knew it. God came to town. How can this be? How could a mere man attract such visibility of the spirits? How did this happen? Simple! Some of these things don't just come by chance, they come to the one prepared for it. Sometimes, God waits to see if He can find a man who would put a knife on his throat and cut off the appetite; a man who would say 'No' to food and all the good stuff from a restaurant or the kitchen. He is looking for a man whose heart is perfect towards Him; one, not given to the lusts and sensual cravings of this world. As God finds such a one; the one adds prayer to this effort and learns how to attract God with a good heart; then you see God visiting. God surely comes to town to abide in such a heart and work His schemes out on men. It is normal with God. To effectively attract God's presence, there is need for us to engage in fasting and prayers.

Fasting is a Christian discipline. It is abstaining from food and pleasures for spiritual purposes. It stands in parallel distinction to starvation or hunger strike. It is also different from health dieting, which stresses abstinence from food but for physical not spiritual purposes. That is to say that every Christian fasting must be for spiritual purposes and must therefore be backed by prayer. Thus we often hear of prayer and fasting. This is because any fasting without prayers is just starvation. It is also worthy of note that fasting is not exclusively a Christian discipline. All the other religions of the world recognize and practice fasting.

Fasting must forever center on God, not just on the blessing and benefits. It must be God-initiated and God ordained. God questioned the people in the days of Zechariah – "When you fasted... did you at all fast unto me" (Zechariah 7:5). If our fasting is not focused on God, it is not acceptable and therefore ineffective.

Fasting can unravel many undesirable things in us. This is a wonderful benefit to the disciple who desires to be transformed into the image of Jesus Christ. If pride controls us, it will he unraveled almost immediately. David said 'I humble my soul with fasting". Anger, bitterness, jealousy, strife, fear will come to lime-light during fasting. We can rejoice in this knowledge because we know that healing for the soul is available through the power of Christ.

Fasting helps us to keep our balances in life. How easily do we allow non-essentials to take precedence in our lives? How quickly we crave for things we do not need until they enslave us. Paul wrote "All things are lawful for me, but not all things are expedient, all things may be expedient but I cannot be brought under the power of any" I pommel my body and subdue it. Likewise David wrote: "I afflicted myself with fasting (Psalm 35:13).

In fasting we discipline the flesh and give the Spirit freedom to operate.

Fasting can be summarized to include, but not limited to, doing the following: (Isaiah 58:1-12)

- to lose the bands of wickedness;
- to undo the heavy burdens and let the oppressed go free;
- to break every yoke; to deal (give) our bread to the hungry;
- to bring the poor that are cast out to your house;
- when you see the naked that yon may cover him and not hide from him.

The result of above obedience is unprecedented. Summary of the values of fasting include increased effectiveness in intercessory prayer, guidance in decision, increased concentration, deliverance from demonic bondage, physical well-being, revelations from the word of God.

Fasting must be God-centered and not for drawing attention of others (Matthew 6:16-18). No disciple can do without fasting because there are some spiritual tasks that cannot be accomplished except by prayer and fasting.

4. YOU ARE JAZZED TO BE ZEALOUS

Oke Oba, Agege area in Lagos was one of the zonal headquarters of our Church. Every first Sunday of the month all the parishes or branches under the zone would hold communion service together. On this fateful evening, the Choir was set for their special rendition. The Choir Master was ready. The Choir was dressed up, poised for something different. We were seated at the altar, each minister with his assigned duty for the 90 minute service. One female voice echoed an alto, other members of the group followed with irritant energy from what could have been mistaken as fueled from an energy drink. There was silence. Again the female voice thundered. Then the echo. Another silence. With the directors' control stick in hand, the Choir Master swung to action. Members fixed their gaze on him as though they would sing with their eyes. With every move, every wave, the choir sang. His head denoted some tones, his arm controlled a segment of the group from the main orchestra. As the Choir sang under his direction, every syllable fitted to his instruction especially with intermittent pauses and echoes. As the song lasted, it was obvious that the man was the driver of both the song and those who sang. The style, syllable and rendering came together with near perfection. The Lord was in that song as he controlled and directed. At a point, he got into the music, with arms stretched to full length, neck bent towards an expected tremble fill, his other hand beckoning for the middle row response; the man was in the music. His coat soaked with sweat from the 98 degrees (F) heat of tropical Africa. The song was on and the entire congregation stood in acclamation. The Holy Ghost was ready to do His job that faithful evening. I sat in my place thinking the pack of blessings the Father would heap on my brother, the Choir Master. As I thought, he got the more energized, pulled a high note and the choir was on atop again. The auditorium went agog. This time, he was soaked, dripping and in a snap of time, he pulled his coat to add to the instrument with which he directed his crew. To my Choir master, nothing mattered at that time except to produce the best rendition to God. He was ready to use anything and everything to make music for God. He was consumed in it. His life depended on it. He was sold out to God and at that meeting, God was present. I sat with much lessons learned: that zeal for the work was expressively patented that evening. The Lord was glorified in the service that evening.

    Zeal is a very strong factor in the building of a disciple. A disciple can be forgiven if he does not display outstanding physical prowess, or if he does not possess great mental ability, but he cannot be excused if he does not have zeal. If his heart is not aflame with a red-hot passion for the Savior, he stands defeated. The zeal of the disciple puts him to action. It invigorates his spirit never to stay at ease in Zion. Zeal fires back at a time when flesh suggests a 'time off' the work of the Master; when offenses come from even the most trusted in the ministry. Jesus attested the zeal of John the Baptist when he said, "He was a shining and burning light." John 5:35. The extent to which we apply our energies and zeal to the Lord's business testify, to a large degree, how deep the relationship with HIM is. Though we have some misplaced zeal, (Uzi and the sons of Aaron) Numbers 10:1-10 but a good number of kings, prophets and priests were very zealous for the Lord. Paul said "Woe is me if I preach not the gospel."

GO, TELL A FRIEND WHAT HAPPENED TO YOU

In journalism, bad news is good news, they say. In the kingdom of God where we experience this electrifying jerk in the Holy Ghost; where we 'suddenly' turn from sinners to saints, enjoying the goodies of heaven and all the peace and chastity, we know that this experience is good news. Here, good news is good news; and this good news, if not shared, paints a bad image of us. We begin to look like ingrates, selfish and undone folks. We seem to be saying, if we hoard this good news, "We are not really into this thing, we are yet to get the import and the significance." But my state of mind since I signed into the love relationship with Jesus Christ will not let me go away with the experience I have gained. I cannot go away unnoticed because I have something inside that boils up with joy unspeakable. I have a bunch of living water flowing and it must flow to someone around me. This living water is the Holy Ghost and His gifting. So whenever I have the opportunity I engage someone in a discussion, talking about my love affair with Jesus. I want the same to be your preoccupation and passion. In fact I will be alarmed if this is not your call on evangelism and witnessing. Except something did not take place, or something has gone wrong with this experience, that joy must flow. Life should exude out of you at each and every moment. You remember, you are an epistle (letter) written to the hurting world.

Maybe you are shy at talking or engaging folks about something exciting or you are not just cut out to get into people with a story. Not to worry, there is a way to do it. Just be careful to play the game. Watch out for an opening into the person that may want your attention on anything. Be personable and cheerful. Start with a warm embrace and a greeting. He may begin with the football game last weekend or the politics over the week or something in the news. That's a great start. Play the game very well and be engaged. Look out for an opening where a love story can be told or some important angle to humanity need be expressed. Bring in Jesus there. Tell your story.

In witnessing we use the most profound and effective tool to tell the message of God's love and salvation. We use the language of love and a heart of compassion (Matthew 9:36-38, Luke 19:10). Prayers are inevitable and of course the word of God. The need to bring the lost sinner into the fold (followers of the Lord Jesus Christ) is imminent and must be done with great care and urgency. It is clear evidence that the world is fast winding up as the futility of human wisdom has failed to meet man's needs. Therefore there is a necessity laid upon every Christian to preach the gospel of our Lord Jesus Christ. Paul said "Woe is me if I preach not the gospel; and the preacher says, "the fruit of righteousness is a tree of life, and he that wins soul is wise" (Proverbs 11:30). "But you shall receive power after the Holy Ghost is come upon you; and ye shall be witnesses unto me..." Acts 1:8

Discussion:
a) What are the methods you may employ to witness to your friends and relations?
b) Make a list of five (5) colleagues, ten (10) friends and ten (10) relations who do not know Jesus Christ as their Lord and Savior or who are at cross roads with Him.
c) Invite them over for dinner, share a moment with them or watch a movie telling a scriptural story; suggest a prayer and/or church service

on Sunday after the dinner. For kids, form a Bible Club (don't forget the cookies to go along side).
d) Always end with an invitation to accept the Lord Jesus as personal Lord and Savior.

Alternatively, let us try the Jesus' style on the woman of Samaria in John 4:1-26

Strategy 1: Jesus was very tired from the journey, Judea to Galilee; had to pass through Samaria. Just be the Human Being Jesus was. We assume you're tired from work. But God has a purpose in your friend or relation you are with. Go the extra mile, engage in this conversation with your neighbor or colleague.

Strategy 2: Jesus started witnessing with the present circumstance 'water'. Use the language your audience understands, what matters to him/her most; the soft spot.

Strategy 3: Jesus broke the cold war of relationship between the Jews and Samaritans. He was simply a radical revolutionist. Sometimes you have to hit the matter head-on as you are led by the Holy Spirit. Just imagine raising the issue of Republicans and Democrats in an election year in the USA? Be wise in your choice of topic for discussion.

Strategy 4: "Give me to drink." Jesus came to the same level with the woman, identifying with her on her care-about. Use the following tools: Language; Food; Culture; Economy; Business...

Strategy 5: Jesus employed a Q&A principle. There was no preaching, just talk it over; get the person interested in the discussion.

Strategy 6: Jesus was sure of His assertion and was ready to defend them. For effectiveness, you must be armed with your evidences and convincingly put them across. Are you sure of your salvation experience. Put that in a story format and 'sell' your idea.

Strategy 7: Jesus operated in the power and used the gift of the Holy Spirit and word of knowledge. The Holy Spirit has a role to play in the conversion. So we learn to depend on the Holy Spirit to give us insights and direction on the need in the lives we talk to. Imagine that: seven husbands in one life. Trust the Holy Spirit as you witness.

GET CLOSER; ENJOY THE WARMTH NO ONE CAN REFUSE

During winter, heating bills are necessary tickets that must be paid so we can continue to enjoy warmth inside the house or Church or the Community Center. Staying together in a family setting provides warmth and some aura of intimacy. This intimacy ensures that no one member of the home is left behind in any scheme or project. Life is at its best on this platform.

The Lord wants us to hold fellowship together and be there for one another. Knowing that there are so much darts thrown at the believer from the outside, He provides a place of succor and relief for the aching soul. This is the place of fellowship. Getting together and getting involved soothes aches, provides a warmth for prayers and communion. In this large house called Church, God has raised help for diverse and many people from all extractions of life. The place of fellowship is a place of rest and peace. Church can be fun if you want it to be. Assuming it is not, for now, ask your pastor for what can be done to fill this need. Get involved.

Inside the walls of a Church, you'd find the maimed, the depressed, the abused, the happy and the unhappy. There are dejected and confused folks. Whatever the problem, you will find it there. Then you come and let's figure out what can be done to fix these problems. It is also a house of prayer. But in all, it is the house of God. There you find healing and succor. The Holy Spirit is also present to help. So in this jazzed up life, you would always go up to the house of the Lord for worship and prayers. Nothing comes in-between. Not even your online Church. You need some warmth from fellow believers, not from your mobile device or your laptop or personal computer. I am talking about real relationship with real people. Do not despise the gathering of God's people as some people have already started doing; they claim there are no such thing as a Church with walls. Of course there is. Look out for one around you, go and be a part the Church. You will be welcome there.

7. SEE SOMETHING BIGGER THAN YOU

The invitation you received; "Come unto me all ye that are heavy laden.... and I will give you rest...my yoke is easy and my burden is light" is a complete package from the Father through Jesus Christ. And the Father means every word of that promise. It is akin to "In my Father's house, there are many rooms; I go to prepare a place for you in heaven, for where I am there you will also be." Beyond the earthly gains and good life here, the Father promises a paradise. It is dwelling in the presence of the Father... eternally. And as you know, in His presence, there is fullness of joy; there is peace unspeakable and life lived at its fullest. So the Father has something bigger than we can figure out with our human brains or imagine in our limited thoughts. There is a glory awaiting as many as believe this simple, but expensive gospel. It is bigger than you. So in our daily walk with Him, it becomes imperative that we have a vision of heaven and think towards an eternal home, not made with hands or woods or bricks. The book of Revelations gives us an idea of the stuff the road ways are made of: made of gold.

The things we see around should not becloud our vision of heaven. I want to encourage you to run to the finish line. Set your gaze at heaven and do everything within given grace to abide with God in glory. Then will we have the right attitude towards earthly vision and pursuit. While still here, we give ourselves to visions that occupy us with heaven's programs and purposes.

The use of the word 'vision' in scripture is largely associated with seeing things that God decides to show an individual while wide awake or sleeping. We may be tempted to conclude that Biblical visions are revelations of God's mind and/or purposes. Here, we want to broaden the concept a little further to include having a sense of direction, having goals and objectives. For example,

- The prophet saw 'an almond tree'
- The man born blind saw men walking like trees
- Daniel saw the salvation reserved for nations

In the physical, a number of ambitions can be referred to as personal visions or goals. Divine vision is not just personal goals, but a revelation by God about His plan and program for the individual or a group. It is a task to be accomplished.

Comprehensive revelations can be a chain of four hooks or a component of four elements. These are:

- Vision of God (Isaiah 6:1); Genesis 12;15; 17; 28:10-19
- Vision of Self (Isaiah 6:5); Job 42:1-6
- Vision of Others (Isaiah 6:5); 1 Peter.1:22-25
- Vision of Task/Commission (Isaiah 6:8); Acts 9:15&16

We learn from these that:
  a) The content of the message was not made known to Isaiah until after his response. So when you seek the full context of a vision or instruction given to you, sometimes it comes only when you have gone into executing the project or at least made an entry into the execution process.
  b) Each Christian disciple has a function to perform in the Body of Christ. Ephesians 4:7-12: Romans 12:3-8. That tells you that there is room for everyone.
  c) It is possible for every Christian to know his/her vision. This is because God does not want us to walk in the dark and ignorance. Amos 3:7
  d) God does not force visions upon people. That is why He asked, "Whom shall 1 send and

who will go for us." If you are waiting for God to compel you to do what you know you should do, you may wait for eternity.

DISCUSS WITH A FRIEND

Consider a 5-year plan for your local church/fellowship. How do you see the vision of God in it? What aspect of the vision do you think is:

1. for yourself? 2. for others? 3. for eternity? 4. or tasks/ job to be done? Do you have a vision of what God wants you to do for life? God wants men of vision; He wants men who can fulfill their vision in mission; those who can execute their visions.

Chapter 4.

DEVELOP A THIRST FOR REALITY

It is possible to live through life, realizing your dreams; especially if God is in them. The Spirit of God provides the force or power to make those dreams come through. He who believes, out of his belly shall flow rivers of living waters. Do you believe that God can do the impossible in your life? Do you know that the everlasting God, the Lord of all the Earth is able to do, according to His words of promise? Jesus said "All things are possible to him who believes."

Your dream is a quantum of desires and aspirations within the ambit of spiritual seclusion. It is a race into the world of 'may be' and an expectation of the birth of a vision. When God gives a dream, He expects that dream to be realized especially, the type that is in consonance with the word and the will of God. Most of the times, we may want to check out our dreams with the word of God and the testimony and counsel of elders. Dreams and visions are sometimes a product of the heart and the occupation of the busy mind. However, God reveals His mind to the elect through dreams and visions. A quest into the mind of God on any given issue validates and assures the Christian that he is a son indeed. This quest into spiritual engagement is the focus of this chapter and it is my prayer that the Lord will develop a deep thirst and hunger for His glory as we study along.

There are many Churches and ministries and ministers all over, doing the work of God; even in the face of looming needs. It is also interesting to note that God is still searching for men. Truly, there is a draught of men and there seems to be very few men God is able to squeeze out and trim and train for the work. I dare say that despite all the 'noise' and flamboyant display of programs, there has not been a complete filling to the great commission. There are a lot of vacant positions yet to be filled. He said: "Lo I searched for men and I found none, not one worthy"... "my eyes run to and fro the earth looking for a man whose heart is perfect towards me".... and none is able to open the scroll in heaven and on earth, no, not one among men... When God gets hold of a man in any generation, then you know revival begins. He is in search of men of reality and truth. In His search for a man in any community or nation (peoples group); and until He finds one; then He is able to conquer kingdoms and institutions. I know there are basic prerequisites God has laid out for any man that will fill this use. Until then, our pursuit for joy and glamorous things would amount to nothing. We will be occupied with frivolities of "how much is in my bank account" or "what type of house I have built" and such physical encumbrances to the detriment of reality and life itself. I have taken time to think about our present practice of faith. Here are a few nuggets from my thought library:

I discover that there is abundant supply of men and women who think they are prepared but unfortunately are NOT. They glazed through a certain knowledge about God and had a brush with an introductory miracle. True, these all came from God but they were not simply prepared for the work of the ministry. These men were not trimmed, were not trained by the HOLY SPIRIT. They needed a touch of FAITHFULNESS; proved and tried in the school of FAITH and enabled to stay the course and come out with testimonies of long suffering through trials and toughness as they do the work in their small, little corners. Another group need to make themselves AVAILABLE. They are not just there to hear or listen to the voice of the Holy Ghost. They are busy, trading and making money with the gospel. Majority of such folks need to learn commitment, surrendered life and a resignation of self and all conjugal attachment to the world. Availability is making oneself visible and always willing to say "Lord here I am, use me." A closer walk with God through a mentor produces results. The Christian man gains wisdom and experience by not staying 'afar off'; he gains traction and poise. He/she learns fast. Another group are not just TEACHABLE or OBEDIENT. This is the rare quality of subjecting oneself to being taught and corrected. Arrogance, pride and high self esteem have been the cancer eating many a Christian up, especially in the Western world. There is no end to learning for any man that must be used by God. Everyone, preacher or Pastor or Bishop ought to have a mentor or an instructor.

At the Garden of Gethsemane Jesus came to a point where He begged the Father to take the cup away from Him. If we get to that stage where we know God as we should, we will also be able to say, Father not my will but thine will be done. If you are going to be in this endtimes army, it is certain that some of us may be sent to prison; some to death in order to save nations. God has His plans. He will not come until every kindred, kingdom, tongue and nation is represented in His Kingdom. (Revelations 5:9-10)

When the word becomes so scarce such that the High Priests cannot hear and preach the voice of God again, God will choose a Samuel. We cannot wait until we know Him completely before we begin to do His work - We are His work-in-progress. For Noah, the instruction he was given, to the natural man, sounded foolish (Genesis 6:13-22). Abraham was asked to offer his son as sacrifice even though God has said that murder was forbidden. Do you think Abraham understood the details? He didn't. But did he obey? He completely did. (Genesis 22:1-19) Philip was having a wonderful crusade in Samaria, Acts 8; and God didn't even give him time to conclude the crusade. But God asked him to go to the desert. He didn't understand but obeyed. This is because the purpose for his life is not to hold one city wide crusade but that through him, light will come to Africa. Acts 8:5-8, 26-40.

In first Kings chapter seventeen and second Kings chapter two we find Elijah; was jealous for God. He was, above all, an obedient prophet. The brook and birds brought food to him, in I Kings 17:3-7. God said that he should go to a widow. A prophet to go to a widow? I Kings 17:9-16. In another instance God commanded the prophet; "Go and show yourself to the king" I Kings 18:1. This was the king who later wanted to kill him. Why must

God send his prophet to such a deadly mission? The take away here is not to fully understand 'reasons' why God does His own program in a useful life, but the OBEDIENCE of men who followed God with no questions asked. However I see something common to all the people who obeyed God and followed. They saw something of eternal value, beyond the cosmos and the ephemeral appeals of this world. They saw glory in the heavens. They saw something bigger than their visions and dreams. As a result, they were not mindful of the scams on Earth. They were sold out to what they saw and were pursuant to these; were determined to meet the mark; to brace the tape of the finish line. Even where they were offered alternatives, to let go of the kingdom in sight, they chose death (the quick passage to eternity) than those offerings. They held on to their faith in God.

WHY WERE THEY ABLE TO OBEY GOD ALL THE WAY?

The answer to the question is 'faith'. They had a resounding faith that God cannot plan evil for them. I can hear Isaiah echoed, as he was laid between two logs of tree from Lebanon, ready to be sawn into two with jigsaw blades, saying "He loves me and I love Him, whatever happens, it will end well" (Hebrews 11:7- Noah, Hebrews 11:17-19).

God is interested in folks who will go all the way with Him in absolute obedience and reverence. Faith is needed in this effort and engagement. God is still searching for a man after His heart. A man that will mean well to heaven and the course of Jesus: to raise the band of soldiers and occupy until He comes back to Earth. You just need to be faithful in the little you do in your Church or Community; be available for the call of duty and learn to take corrections; ready to obey at all times, even at the expense of your pleasure.

Case Study:
You heard a voice telling you to go for missions. Currently, you belong to a local Church and have a lucrative job perhaps as a medical doctor; and more, you are the bread winner for the immediate and extended family. The urge is deep and voice very clear. Your fiancée is not excited and your parents think you have gone crazy. But then, you must obey the call to a specific mission mandate.

This is also true of a disciple. To help you align well with God's will, you start by asking these basic questions: Why am I in the world? What is God's plan for me? What exactly is my role in the overall plan? How can I achieve what God has in stock for me? Very few people get answers to these questions immediately. You may use this format to get started. God's calling must be accompanied with the following five-P's: Discover your five-P's and guard them carefully.

1. Purpose: This is the life line and specific ministry you are called into. Check the 5 fold ministries in Ephesians 4:11-13. Gal. 1:1-3. Make sure you know God is calling. Don't jump into it.

2. Plan: Get your strategies right with the Holy Spirit as your boss. Itemize your settings, your structures and strategies. Develop a case for your Being; your Calling. What is it that you intend to add to the value heaven is looking for; WHAT VALUE ARE YOU BRINGING ON TO THE TABLE? Differentiate your offering and stand out with a mission.

3. Platform: Where is your pulpit? What concentration area may we look out for you? Is it at the Church, outer missions without walls; in organized groups, institutions; the Mentally Retarded Development Disabilities (MRDD) Homes; the prisons or hospitals. Area of operation; your environment, your catchment niche.

4. People: Who are your audience? What target people groups are you reaching out to? This will help in designing your Plan.

5. Pipes & Conduits: What are your channels of distribution? What materials do you need for the project? What skill-sets and trainings do you have or need to ensure fruitful results and that the ultimate desire of heaven is met. Who are you likely to collaborate and partner with?

Ministry and any other form of engagement require constant reviews and evaluations. Should there be a diminishing marginality in expected output (output here is not limited to tangible, physical gains but tends to include faithfulness, saved souls, increase in the knowledge of the word of God; changed lives for Jesus etc) then I would suggest the following measures be taken to avert collapse.

Review, Restock, Re-strategize, Relaunch... Re-bounce.

In all circumstances and over-all goal is to add value and bring about a change in how things are done. When a red is flagged in ministry operations or vision, there is usually the tendency to throw in the towel and call it quits. Or sometimes the Monday blues come upon the man of God, when a review of Sunday's sermon does not seem to fit; when results and strategies look rusty or mundane. The clogs seem to gather around your once vibrant calling and begin to eat up the very fabrics of your unbending resolve to serve the Lord who saved you with a mighty and strong hand. At such moments you are nose-diving into pity and self defeat. A sense of "it's all over" comes heavily weighted on you. Here, economists would say your Marginal Productivity is negative. May I tell you that it is not over yet; Yes, you may have fallen short but you are not short of the grace and mercy of God. David said, though I fall seven times, yet will I rise again. Here is again my offer:

1. Review your actions and projects. Be careful you are not misquoting God. Check your last call in Prayer and studious search of the word of God and witnessing about His goodness or even what's been revealed.

2. Re-strategize: Revisit Bethel. This is the house of God. Discover whether the trend you used is still in vogue in today's technology driven world. Always review and check your original design, your masterpiece from God as it was delivered to you from the beginning; that original prototype from God upon which every other thing has been built; Check to see if Jesus Christ is being magnified and worshipped. He is the hub in the wheel. Be sure that God is the central point of focus, not you or the air of importance that have blown across your way by reason of exploits and vantages. Remember that the Holy Spirit is a gentle Personality. Do you still honor Him?

3. Now you can begin some asset mapping. Begin by rebranding and employing the strategy of adding values and flavor to what you used to do; get some more training and get to review your 5Ps. Find out new life-styles to your people and their needs and preferences. Match that with what God wants to fix in their lives; what the need is (this is their core needs and value preferences). Anything outside the need of the people (example dealing with sin and seeking for revival), would reduce ministry to a mere project. If ministry does not meet people at their points of spiritual needs, there might be the experience of negative marginal productivity.

4. Re-align the pipe and the conduit. It could be a switch to high tech or a new strategy of using technology to meet a wider reach; example of witnessing and mentoring using facebook or Twitter or the I-cloud communication medium etc. The trick here is to use the right tool at the right time. To understand the trend with people and their preferences

5. Or the new strategy could be entirely a re-engineering of spiritual stimuli. Most times, a clog on the wheel may arise from spiritual oppositions and combatant operations in the realm of the spirit. Because some issues do not go away except by prayer and fasting; albeit, some serious intercessory prayers; there is therefore need to engage in spiritual warfare for the work to move smoothly. (Nehemiah 1, 2, 3...). Spiritual solutions are received on the altar of

PRAYER. There is need to "Pray Until Something Happens" (PUSH) for the enemy of our souls to be brought under our feet. One of our assigned duties as Priests is to pronounce judgment on satanic operations in our homes and ministry. Their influence should not be tolerated, not in any way.

MIRACLES! WHAT'S NEXT?

Before you rush into ministry, please for the sake of sound judgment, read this: "I know a man in Christ who fourteen years ago - whether in the body (or in the spirit) I do not know, or whether in the body or out of the body, I do not know, only God knows... such a one was caught up in the third heaven..... I know he was caught up into Paradise and heard inexpressible words which it is not lawful for a man to utter; of such a one I will boast, yet of myself I will not boast, except in my infirmities...." 2 Corinthians 12:2-5.

In the book of Galatians 1:1, 11-17 Paul clearly stated the process he undertook before launching into public life. First, his fourteen years of solitude and then three years of studying under the apostles suggest to me that God, though is dire need of souls to be saved, would not make a suicidal miscalculation by sending an uninformed, ill-equipped soldier to the war front. Miracles are great; demons must be cast out and the television audience is a big catch as people wait endlessly to catch a glimpse of you and hear your phonology and semantic constructs. Yet, the rule is that "they that wait on the Lord shall renew their strength, they shall run and not be faint, they shall walk and not be weary" Isaiah 40:31.

The nature of man is to obtain instant gratification and feel accomplished as he takes up projects and schemes himself into lime-light. But the plan of God is different. At His set time, after the training and trimming, after a sufficient disclosure of the blue print from heaven, such a man is released to go and truly be God's representative on Earth. Most times, 'undone men' mount the pulpit and begin to offer strange fires unto the Lord. This is spiritual sacrilege. Isaiah 6:1-8 says it all about what the short-cut effect and the lack of revelation can do to a man who seizes the pulpit and begins some self glorification. That is why you need a mentor who can teach you how the run is done; the principles of the kingdom, the purity of life and a sincere persistent occupation in the place of prayer and the word. That is why you must go for fresh fire from an altar that oozes out flames from the Holy Spirit. "And He took coals of fire from off the altar and touched my lips." Fresh fire must come from the altar. The lack of this alter-fire experience leads men to change tactics and begin a callous, embattled soothing story in the name of sermon for their congregation. They engage in story-telling, white-washed, sepulcher-antics that keep large crowds (remember money is the end of all matters in their judgment) gazing and galloping. These are our occupation today. The disciple, true disciple of the Lord Jesus Christ must never engage in these; no, not a man trimmed and trained, tested for heaven's use.

To run with a message, you must receive something divinely ordained. To receive that message, you must wait on God. That waiting and receiving makes you. It launches you into something bigger than you are; something you are willing to die for. Martin Luther King Junior said: "A man is no man if he is not willing to die for what he believes in." And I dare say, if he is not willing to give up all that it takes to obtain all that heaven approves.

Chapter .5.

MY PURPOSE & MY POISE
"The heart of man is deceitful and desperately wicked, who can know it"

When you set out to search for a wife (or the woman begins to have a desire for a man), something tells you that you are mature to reproduce your kind; that you are not an island. You need someone you can pour your life into, some fellowship. This is called 'koinonia' in Greek; means fellowship in our terms.

Recall in Genesis chapter two, where the fellowship with the Father was accessible and cordial. Here the man and the woman were happy, both were naked before each other without any shame. Then consider the unfortunate incident in Genesis chapter three where we see the fall of man; the introduction of knowledge of sin and death; eyes were suddenly opened and fear came upon man. Think about the incidences in heaven recorded far from the reach of time in Isaiah 14:12-17; Ezekiel 28:1- 10. In all these, Satan had a plan and a purpose. He achieved those while playing on the gullible mind of the woman, thereby deceiving Eve.

In all these, God had His plan for man. He made a way to bring him back to Himself (Genesis 3:15) and these started to unfold, albeit, in snippets and various chunks through the ages and dispensations of human development and political life. Until the birth of Jesus Christ, the absolute fulfillment of prophesy was not realized. In summary, we have the following unfolding:

- ❖ There was a great fall and therefore void (vacuum) was created. A position needed to be filled.
- ❖ You will notice that there was DOMINION given to man. But that was traded by man since naturally Satan was not happy about

man's occupation and dispossession of his rights and privileges in heaven.
❖ A plan was put in place by God; the transaction was quick and exact. Jesus showed up and paid and bought man back. And now God is about to enjoy the very reason for which He created man.

My Purpose, Your Purpose

In our age, the age of grace and truth, God has reached out to us by introducing life (through Jesus Christ) and we, on the terms of accepting and believing, are made righteous and have the power to be His sons. By this appointment, we become co-heirs of His kingdom. GOD calls those whom He would. He called the twelve disciples. (Mark 3:13-15). Why?

- So that they could be with Him in fellowship
- To send them forth to preach the gospel
- That they might have power to heal sickness and diseases and to cast out demons

One of the main reasons for the creation of man was God's desire for fellowship (Genesis 1:26). Therefore God made man in His own image so as to enjoy fellowship with Him. (Genesis 3:8&9) God came down to the Garden of Eden to have fellowship with Adam. Therefore, you are made in His image.

Genesis 2:18. God created us to have fellowship with Him; to enjoy an intimacy and closeness that is not orchestrated by the physical provisioning. Nobody is comfortable being alone. God's passion is to hold meetings and communion with us.

In life, when two friends meet, we discover that these things are inevitable:

a) Conversation that is dialogue takes place and there is exchange of ideas. The same is applicable when we meet with God. He says, "come let us reason together..." Isaiah 1:18. Because God respects our humanity and the free will rights He appointed for man, He stoops low to reason with mere man. My poise, your poise should be to engage in a conversation with our Maker.

b) Physical contact - shaking hands, hugging, kissing. Close touch and exact proximity to the Father and the Son provides warmth and a sense of belonging. You may be asking how this happens knowing God is a spirit and we are still here on Earth, physically humans. If you look closely at Matthew 25:34-44 and Isaiah 58:6-9; you will find the place of physical touch in society. Nations and political leaders are also encouraged to kiss the Son by submitting to His authority and terms of governance. Kissing the Son also involves aligning with the Church (body of Christ) to institutionalize righteousness in civil society (a prelude of the things to come in the Millennial reign) and implant righteous and moral values in our societies.

c) Sharing their meals. God also wants to dine with us (Revelation 3:20) for He said "I stand at the door..." fellowship with God is something deep. Communion, love and commitment to one another were the last mandates the Lord Jesus left His disciples with. In communion, we remember the death of our Lord Jesus Christ and all the marred visage we find in His death. We have been enjoined not to forget this sacrament. This is the hall mark of our Christian faith.

d) With real friends, there is always exchange of gifts. "They that wait upon the Lord shall renew (exchange) their strength" Isaiah 40:31. The value Holy Spirit brings into the life of a Christian and all the changes He brings cannot be estimated in dollar terms. When we also think about the death penalty and all the humiliations Jesus suffered for humanity, we can scarcely imagine how much we, humans, can pay back to God. So the real exchange of gifts is not an exchange, rather it is an appreciation; a token that expresses our heart to God. This means that when God asks us to come to His house with an offering, or a tithe, or some thanksgiving token, He merely tests our gratitude. Real friends give away 'anything' to their beloved one. Paul writes, 'do not come to Him with empty hands." The Macedonians gave everything they had even while under a weight of poverty. The union between a man and his wife is so intimate and fused together that the two are fused as one. The same applies to Christ and the Church; so much as there ought not to be a delineating line separating one's wealth from the demands of His Church in pursuing kingdom projects and principles.

e) There will be strengthening of the fellowship. Revelation 3:20. Matthew 11:28:- Come and rest John 7:37; Come and drink Isaiah 1:18 Come and chat with Him.

God's Mandate for Every Useful Life
a) Called to Worship

Before 2017, Koenigsegg isn't a household name in the world of supercars, like Bugatti or Ferrari. It has managed to develop quite a reputation over a short period of time, beating the best supercars in the market. The Agera R model is a perfect example of the brand's might and power that blows all other supercars in the storm with a top speed of over 273 mph, faster than any other supercar you will find on the market today. This is why it's also known as the fastest car in the world currently. The German's Koenigsegg is built for speed. In the same manner, man was created for worship. His gaze was to focus on God and enjoy fellowship and great moments with his Maker. the fruits in the garden were provided to be eaten for strength and energy, never as a substitute or principal focal point in the overall scheme of things. But things have long changed. Fruits and possessions have taken center stages. You are called to worship in everything you do. To worship means to seek and do His will, to obey the word from the Lord and walk in His ways. It also includes to sing praises to the Father; to respect the presence of the Holy Spirit in your body, home and office. When we engage the Father in all we do, (I mean in ALL we do), there is an unhindered flow of His presence. If, on the other hand we have our poise directed at "all we can acquire" "how much fame we can garner" then there is a limited hope for a fulfillment of His mandate for a useful life.

b) Called to serve

In June 1884 the Moody Mission came to an end, and C.T. Studd (1860 - 1931) wondered what to do next, knowing that he had enough money to last him until he was 26. At 26, he was to inherit enough wealth to live comfortably for the rest of his life. As a result he did not need to get into business or engage in a professional career and his thought turned towards thousands of people who were dying every day without the gospel. One evening a friend gave Studd a tract written by an atheist. In the tract the atheist explained what he would do if he really thought Christianity was true as many English men in Studd's time claimed to be. C.T. Studd read: If I firmly believed, as millions say they do, that the knowledge and practice of religion in this life influences destiny in another, then religion would mean to me everything. I would cast away earthly enjoyments as dross, earthly cares as follies, and earthly thoughts and feelings as vanity. Religion would be my first waking thought and my last image before sleep sank me into unconsciousness. I should labor in its cause alone. I would take thought for the morrow of Eternity alone. I would esteem one soul gained for heaven worth a life of suffering. Earthly consequences would never stay my hand, or seal my lips. Earth, its joys and its grieves, would occupy no moment of my thoughts..."...I would strive to look upon Eternity alone, and on the immortal souls around me, soon to be everlastingly happy or everlastingly miserable. I would go forth to the world and preach to it in season and out of season, and my text would be, WHAT SHALL IT PROFIT A MAN IF HE GAINS THE WHOLE WORLD AND LOOSES HIS OWN SOUL?"

Yes, the tract had been written to shame Christians for lack of their action, it had the opposite effect on C.T. Studd. It spurred him into action. His legacy remains as a missionary to China, India and Central Africa.[1] We have been saved to serve. The service we render here on Earth is an investment heaven records to our credit. More than an investment, it is a way of giving back to humanity the very gains we have obtained from the Lord. We are supposed to shine as lights to the world and show compassion to those whose destinies have been derailed by Satan.

Service to humanity and the Church ought to be our waking thoughts and sleeping dreams. God's love lights up our environment when we fit our hearts and hands towards meeting needs of hurting people. The world has seen many preachers and bishops. They are waiting for real believers, willing to lift them from pits of despondency to heights of bliss. The things we do speak so loud that they cannot hear the noise from our noise making machines. Leonard Ravenhill muted his heart longing to a few believers with this: "In all thy getting, get unction" Apply your heart and hands to the things that matter.

---

[1] C.T.Studd; "No Retreat" 1958. Youth With A Mission Publishers (an inspiring true story of men and women who answered the call of God

c) **Called to minister life**

We are ministers of the new covenant by the grace of God. Our job is to create environments conducive for a discharge of God's word, truth, mercies and grace to humanity. The world is hurting and we've got healing balms to apply it to the wounds. Sin is endemic in the system. God has called us to go, preach to everyone. Because sin eats a man like cancer does, man is smart to address this sin problem with a wish-wash program that goes away through psychology and gene editing. This is false and demonic. Our lives ought to impact the lives of others around us.

As a Church we ought to provide some value to the people, the number of Churches doting our streets, notwithstanding. For example, the different flavors and forms of Churches ought to provide some new offerings to the body of Christ and to humanity. Assuming you have been asked to float a new Church, ask yourself; what are the things God is requiring of me to add as value to the body of Christ? There are gifting the Church lacks; what are those? How would I position myself as a leader or helper to fulfilling this mandate? Purpose of your local Church is provide warmth, life and succor to the body of Christ and be a blessing to the general society. This is our calling and our occupation.

WHEN GOD VISITS A MAN...
CASE STUDY: ABRAHAM Genesis 18

- Destinies are changed
- Covenants are made
- Life programs are redirected
- Altars are built
- Your will is sub-summed in His will

Then comes the swelling of Jordan

Let us assume you have cried and repented from your sins and lukewarm behavior; that you now know that God is interested in your life and has heavily invested in this life for His glory and praise. You are poised for action. Somehow you still ask:

- ❖ Why is the wicked prospering?
- ❖ Why don't I have much to show after much labor?
- ❖ Why are the heavens not seeded, thus there are no rains? Jeremiah 8:19-22; 9:1&2.

Check out these Scriptures:
Jeremiah 9:23&24; Jeremiah 12:1-5
Psalm 91; Isaiah 64:3 Fear the Lord; Know Him;
Dwell in the presence of God;
Learn to walk (with men), run (with foot men) and ride on horses

Some Areas we can operate in Ministry:
The 5-Fold Ministry (Ephesians 4:11-13; 1 Corinthians 12:28-31)
1. Apostles
2. Prophets
3. Evangelists
4. Pastors
5. Teachers

Others:
1. Helps (Aids) and Volunteerism
2. Administrations/ Governments
3. Charity
4. Elders/ Deacons
5. Community Agents
6. Table Servers
7. Keepers at Gate (Watchmen)
8. Missionaries
9. Sons/ Daughters of Consolation
10. Ministry Helpers/ Sponsors... etc

Sincerely identify the area of your calling and seek God's face as to how you will be involved and committed to it. Share same with your pastor or bishop. You may use the following quadrant as a guide to yourself discovery and personality scaling.

KEEP AN EYE ON THE PRINCIPLES THAT MAKE FOR SUCCESSFUL MINISTRY

Obedience... Come, and he comes; go, and he goes... Matthew 8:5-12; 11:28-30; John 15, then Authority.

Consecration and Sanctification Colossians 3:1-5; Romans 12:1

Commitment   Philippians 3:1-12

Sowing & Reaping   Galatians 5: 23; 6:7

The way up is down Philippians 2:8-11; Acts. 20:38; Luke 6:38

God allows the wheat and the weeds to grow in the vineyard until the end

Love: Having a romantic embrace with God revs your spirit. 2 Corinthians 5:16; Galatians 6:17.

Chapter .6.

SPIRITUAL VICTORY

"Be strong in the Lord and in the power His might..."
Ephesians 6:10

Operation desert storm was a quick and concise one. Military attacks are not mere stooges that come from shallow thinking. They are planned, embellished with trained, astute and combatant ready military personnel. Military Installations are made to fit the terrain and nature of combat and supplies for refills are not lacking. Planned and well-executed operations bring about victories.

The Soldier you are called to be.... 2 Timothy 2:1-5. The disciple is a combatant soldier and not ceremonial one. 2 Corinthians 10:12 – "For we wrestle not against flesh and blood." A disciple is engaged in an intense warfare. Lessons to learn from the passage 2 Corinthians 10:1-12:

- The personality or leader of the opposing gang we are fighting is Satan.
- Satan has a kingdom. His kingdom is not divided against himself.
- The devil is the ruler and the prince of this world.
- He has a highly organized system.
- In the army, there are ranks. In like manner, there are ranks in the kingdom of Satan - demons, witches, principalities, powers, rulers respect themselves. Each of them knows his jurisdiction, Daniel 10:10-13.

Be Strong in the Lord

Soldiers of the kingdom are made; they are not born into the kingdom (a child is born into the home). In Galatians chapter four, we see that heirs of the kingdom, as long as they remain babies are not able to take ownership of their heirs (possessions). They remain children and unable to assess their inheritance. They are not matured to ascend their thrones. Immaturity makes them children though they are supposed to be heirs. To be a soldier you must be called, trained, tested, and trimmed. This is the difficult part... Tell me how? To prepare for combatant operations, what type of life-style is required? (Housing? food? luggage?)

Name your armory and needed skill-sets (use the Roman soldier's tool-kit). Because we belong to a kingdom, our method of operation takes a cue from the kingdom we belong. There are principles and attitudinal behaviors the soldier of this kingdom must abide by. As a matter of fact, God has released us to occupy and institutionalize His original intent for the Earth. God wants us to know the following:

- Living in Dominion is about ruling; about taking authority; about making an impact; about changing destinies... It involves resistance, reigning over, subjugating the evil one, subduing powers, prevailing; living in victory
- That man will be everything on Earth as God is to the Universe
- You can walk in Dominion; just know who you are
- You must have a divine nature (be restored and reinstated with power)

- God is searching for a man who will stop (say NO to the devil)
- Be determined to fight and kill 2 Timothy 2:1-5; 2 Corinthians 10:4-6
- Abide by the rules of war Matthew 11:1-12
- Once signed in, you're locked in (Hebrews 1: 24-29); Luke 9:23-26; 57-61
- Earth and its citizens will hate you Luke 19:12, 15 and 27, 2 Timothy 3:12-15
- You must be focused Luke 9:51; Colossians 4:17; Acts 20:18-24

Final Statements

He stood patiently as the roll call was made. A long queue of believers and pastors and bishops took their turns for the final judgment. God was the arbitrator. The eternal fate of men and women were being decided on and there was silence. A faceless being with a high sounding tone announced the names. Beyond the divide were multitude of souls crying and wailing. A big GULF, oozing flames and fury caged them in as their cries received no response. The roll call went on. Everyone was at a standstill. Speechless; afraid of the next action: to be turned into the flame or go the other side. Fury was in the voice that made the call. As he moved closer, sweat was all over him: a combination of the heat from flame and a worked-up reaction inside of this bishop. His stomach churned as he recalled his stewardship. He took inventory of the life he led as a bishop on Earth; wondered if that would cut the mercy of God. Mercy? It was announced that mercy was no more, had hidden himself, for fear of the fury on God's face. As names pumped into an echo, the Bishop moved closer and was permitted to look into the GULF. His name was skipped. An Angel took him to look into the pit. He did. He saw men wailing and crying like babies. He saw Bishops and Pastors crying for help. He saw a great number of Church Presidents and founders, snatching and wailing. They were visibly alive with their senses intact; they reasoned. He took a long look and saw many more in his congregation who had died and were among the choice elders; those who decided the fate of many in the Church. He saw the poor, the rich and the affluent. He was stunned at those very successful lords who had cut their teeth into the juicy side of life; He saw unimaginable personalities in Hell. He still has their names because he remembers them by name, especially the very popular ones in ministry. The Angel was quick to remind him that he did not belong to their environment. That he needed to go back to Earth to testify to what he saw. And he woke from his sleep, sweating, almost traumatized. This revelation took place in Nigeria through one of the Pastors.

"Then I saw a great white throne and Him who sat on it from whose face the Earth and the Heaven fled away. And there was found no place for them. And I saw the dead, small and great, standing before God, and the books were opened. And another book was opened which is the Book of Life. And the dead were judged according to their works, by the things which were written in the books. And the sea gave up the dead who were in it, and Death and Hades delivered up the dead who were in them. And they were judged, each according to his works." Revelations 20:11-13.

God is watching and will definitely bring to judgment all the works of man. I fear and tremble at his word because God does not regard the status of man. He is the ALMIGHTY GOD, who is able to give life and to kill; to bless and to destroy. As I walk through life and give myself to the work in ministry, I am aware that one day I will stand before the One who appointed me in this enterprise. He warns that all things must be done in purity and holiness, in equity and in righteousness. I fear and tremble. How can anyone be comfortable with sin as one does this work? Behold He comes in the clouds! Please tread softly.

Sometime in 1994 my beloved brother, Engineer Harrison Elekwa lost his wife, Chinenye, through cancer. Prior to her death, she had engaged in Hospital evangelism, ministering to those cancer patients. She was a medical doctor, the best in her class (University of Nigeria Enugu Campus, UNEC) and therefore knew the implications of her disease. It was a painful loss. We grieved and so did Elekwa. About a week after that, the Lord brought her to me in the dream of the night. I asked her why she left us in such a grief. I knew she was in heaven so I asked "what day of the week is it over there?" She replied: "I don't know because everything is bright here; there is no night, no darkness, no pain, no sorrow, everything is perfect." "Please go tell my husband to stop crying and living in grief. You people should strive to come to where I am." With that the Lord took her away, and I woke up. I went up to Elekwa and relayed the message. He was consoled.

I write to inform you that the Lord will soon appear to check on what you did with your life. True, most people came this way (Western world) for a better life, to make wealth and gain some relief in life. That's wonderful and reassuring to know. The bottom-line is the end-game. The ultimate resurgence of your soul; where you and I will wake up on the other side of the divide.

IT IS A SERIOUS MATTER

"Nevertheless the solid foundation of God stands; having this seal: The Lord knows them that are His and let everyone that names the name of Christ depart from iniquity" 2 Timothy 2:19 KJV. It does not matter who you are, whether you are a General Overseer, or a Bishop or a Pastor or a Minister or a member of the Church, I reiterate that God is not a respecter of persons. He's got no grand children and so will mete out judgment on evil perpetrators, your position and title, notwithstanding. Every man's works will be tested by fire. On the Day of Judgment, all works and ministerial engagements will be revealed (hidden and open) and if you have built with woods and stubbles God's fire will consume them all. It is only the thing that was built with gold that will stand. All others will be consumed by fire. What are you building with?

David walked up and requested that he may tell me something when I come back from work. That's unusual with him because, we know in the family, God has given us the ability to be expressive and bare out issues off the mind. So I wondered why the wait until evening. He asked me to wait. I did. After dinner, he opened up, "Dad, it seems that the world will soon come to end, that Jesus will soon come" "Why do you say that?" I inquired. "Last night I saw some things I could not understand. Angels flying in the clouds and announcing the arrival of Jesus. The whole place was in confusion and everyone was hyper and seemed to be running from themselves. People did not know what to do because, it was like judgment was coming. After sometime I woke up." I remember explaining the revelation and encouraged him to keep the faith and continue in prayers; that he is a privileged son to receive such a revelation from God. And that was David, my teenage boy. For out of the mouth of sucklings God has ordained truth and praise. "For the Lord Himself will descend from the heaven with a shout, with the voice of an archangel, and with the trumpet of God; and the dead in Christ will rise first. Then we who are alive and remain shall be caught up together with them in the clouds to meet the Lord in the air. And so shall we always be with the Lord" 1 Thessalonians 4:16&17 KJV.

Adrian is a preacher of the word of God here with us in Cincinnati Ohio. When the Lord set His hand on his life, Adrian has this to say: "I saw the Lord in a vision of the night and He commissioned me into the Ministry, (a reminiscent of the finger of God) over the years with instructions to go and tell the world about His Son, Jesus Christ." Adrian continues: '' I was taken up in the spirit realm to an isolated, but familiar location. Thereafter, spectacular beams of light came from the cloud (heavens) and suddenly, there appeared the right hand of a man radiating such an intense light from the cloud and wrote this life changing mandate - "GO YE and PREACH THE GOSPEL. I AM COMING SOON."

Thereafter, the hands that wrote these words in the cloud disappeared gradually from my view, back into the cloud (heavens). Ever since then, God has been faithful to His words in my life to the Nations."

Again I was in another world. It was celestial and pristine, sparkling with unapproachable LIGHT; it was providing brightness and illumination to every corner. The homes are well built, great habitation for everyone. Streets were paved with something that made them glitter and shine. I was told it was gold. There were no cars or trucks or planes. No food, nothing you can hold on to. Nothing that we use or cling to here on earth. But everything was perfect. Everyone extremely happy and at peace, playing as kids do. We were just babies, checking out our rooms and just having great moments and suddenly a voice spoke to me: "You are a pastor, where are the members of your congregation?" Immediately I started a serious search for our members in the midst of many people: white, black, all nations and tongues represented. As I searched, I saw one brother. I exclaimed "Praise God, you made it to heaven... thank God!" And he joined me in the search... and in the course of this important search; I was brought back to Earth. I found one brother...just one. This bothers me as a pastor. And indeed I am in pain.

Would you join me to check our last encounter with the lover of our souls, to discover where we have missed it and return to Him again? The Lord is rich in mercy, always willing to forgive and prop up where there is a decay, where latency has caged our souls and there seems to be an "Ichabod" written all over our altars. The glory of the Most High is not withdrawn, no, it is still available to as many as would take advantage of the flowing stream of mercy. The power of the Holy Spirit is still at work in our generation and God is waiting for a response from us.

As a student of the School of Disciples, which path will you follow on this journey? The path of honor and glory in the work you are training to do; to serve with diligence of purpose; striving to the end with no stain on your garment? Or will you engage in frivolities of life, pursuing the earthly wealth and acceptance from those who already signed in for hell and destruction? You see, the altar you so much cherish can perfect you. If you go for true fire that purifies, the anointing of the Holy Spirit typified by holy character, if you really want to pursue to know Him (His nature and character) and thus be like Him, the Lord will reveal Himself to you. You will know Him. But the other side is one you would not want to engage in. As you know, the power of the altar and insurgence of the lure from it, grants you some measure of immunity. You seem to be above rebuke. You are the lord now, over God's people and so if unchecked, you think you are on the right path. Sin creeps in and is re-baptized or renamed. It rolls on the heels of modern slang and nothing is done about it. Be careful! Do you know as you approach the end of this book and want to go into ministry, some thoughts on how you will build the biggest Church in town surges in your mind? The quest to have a very big and rich Church membership keeps you thinking about the location of your hive; and the glamour and 'glory' of your tabernacle. Wait a minute; that is not the essence of ministry; that is not your calling. You have even printed some big posters with your face announcing the arrival of 'Bishop XYZ' in town (remember a bishop is a superintendent of a legion of Churches) and yet you just begun. When you rev your car, the first sound of the engine gives you an idea of how far the car will go.

Your foundation speaks a lot about your occupation in ministry: whether you are cut for filthy lucre or you mean well to heaven and all its witnesses. It is this faulty foundation that is the problem today. Will you cause heaven to smile again and God boast about your ministerial appointment? Even in the face of filth and decay, there is hope; the hope of REVIVAL. You are a tool in His hands; a battle cry of heaven to undo the bands of wickedness and re-establish righteousness and equity in our land. You can sign in and be of great use in God's hand. To eschew filth and decay; to say NO to sin (marrying and remarrying and yet cling to the altar; cutting corners with tax papers and forging every document so that you can gain it all; using your marketing gimmicks to extort money from people in the name of fund raising; fornicating and committing adultery right there in the Church; being complacent about the sin of homosexuals and lesbians; of blatant display of tribalism and racial discrimination in the house of God, yet you pose as a pastor? The list goes on and on.). Can you join me to say NO to these, even when they lure you with so much money and TV adverts. Remember your home country (heaven) which you represent; to be a true disciple of Jesus Christ; an ambassador of heaven. When you sign up for your assignment, give heed to these things and please occupy until the return of our Master.

MARANATHA! GET JAZZED! BE INSPIRED! LET US PRAY!

Chapter .7.

TRAINING FOR THE CHRISTIAN WORKER
(A Training Course at Dominion Center, Cincinnati Ohio)

INTRODUCTION

The goal of the training include the following:
1. To prepare and enlist mature group of believers who will be able to walk, work with and teach others the gospel (good news) at the least, and sufficiently lead those to Christ

2. To get believers, efficient and able to teach scripture and reproduce disciples who can stand on their own to make disciples of others

3. To prepare workers for the Church with the knowledge in administration, logistics, management and finances so that they will make effective use of resources in chosen areas of service. Others include Choristers, ushers, evangelism, media, engineering / maintenance etc.

It is expected that a believer who is undergoing Workers Training must have undergone Believers Class or New Converts Class and Baptismal Class and has been baptized. Therefore a worker in training should know what assurance of salvation is; solutions to struggles about his faith, able to defend his new found faith and be prepared, with eagerness to advance with Christ in his daily living. He / She is studying the Word of God unhindered.

WHO IS A WORKER?

He is a born again child of God; renounced the unholy things of this world and has denied the lusts, ephemeral and mundane things of the world. He is a believer, expected to be zealous and ready to work for God (John 14:12). The Christian worker has a mandate to accomplish and have specific action plan towards meeting the goals and missions of the Church.

However, a worker would have been chosen and dedicated for a particular service (Luke 17:1-19). He has the vision of heaven and sees the need to work together with other leaders of the Church so that he can achieve the set goals of the general assembly of the body of Christ as well as fulfill the God-given mandate of his life.

In a simple way, a worker has seen the need to work together with others to help achieve the goals of the Church which are to witness, win souls, encourage, support, and build people (emotionally, professionally, socially and at family levels) while getting them mature in Christ. He is also preparing them for the second coming of our Lord Jesus Christ.

PRINCIPLES OF AN ASPIRING WORKER

Principle is a fundamental truth or proposition that serves as the foundation for a system of belief or behavior or as a chain of reasoning or argument. It is a rule governing one's personal behavior. In our study, a principle is a fundamental or general truth that makes up and guides a worker in his service. It is the essence of the worker, the standard or rules of his personal convictions and conduct.

Life principles are truths that can be derived from Scriptures. They are many and thus cannot be taught in this single training slot but we advise that as a worker advances and matures in his / her services, he/ she will come to understand them more. However for the purposes of this training, we will discuss ten courses which will include:

1. What must I do to be enlisted to work for God?
2. What will YOU have me do, Lord?
3. I love my Lord so I must work the work
4. I am a part of His family so I must finish the work
5. The enemy is not happy, so I am engaged in a fight
6. Got the sword and the word; I must make an impact
7. My work will be tested
8. I've made a decision to be a team player
9. My expectation will not be cut off, there's a pay day!
10. My department, the job description; I'm set to go!

Course 1: What must I do to be enlisted to work for God? John 6:28&29

The question alludes to what qualifies one to be enlisted in the work? The Lord Jesus Christ gave an answer (v29) which summarizes as "believe." To do God's work, the Christian worker must believe in God. To believe is to accept the offer of salvation; His personality, doctrine and Word. To believe is to have faith in God's ability to do what He says He will do and entrust your whole frame (spirit, soul and body) on Him. To believe is to accept. What then should you accept?

Offer of His salvation Titus 2:9-11; Acts 4:12
Jesus personality, which includes the following:
He is the way, the truth and the life John 14:6
The good Shepherd John 10:11, 14
The resurrection John 11:25
The light of the whole world John 9:5
The door John 10:7
The true vine John 15:1
Jesus, the Son of God John 10:36
Jesus, as the Lord and Master John 13:13
Jesus, one with the Father John 10:30; 17:20-26
The Messiah John 4:26
The Alpha and Omega Revelations 1:8, 17
Accept the doctrine of Jesus Christ.

Every Church has a fundamental doctrine which is also called the apostolic doctrine. Members, especially the workers are expected to accept and abide by and defend (Hebrews 6:1-3) these doctrines. The doctrine of a local Church must be in sync with the doctrine of our Lord Jesus Christ, thus it is apostolic.

These are:

The doctrine must be of God (To preach Righteousness, Holiness, Sanctification, Consecration etc) John 7:16-18

Must be scriptural 2 Timothy 3:14-17 (Water Baptism, Restitution, Resurrection, Miracles, 66 Books of the Bible, Baptism of the Holy Spirit, Trinity as in God the Father, God the Son and God the Holy Ghost as one)

The word of God is used to exhort and convict. Titus 1:7-9 (Rapture of the Church; Millennial Reign of Christ, New Heaven and New Earth; Hell Fire

It is for teaching. 2 Timothy 4:1-5

Abhors any other doctrine 1 Timothy 1:8-10

The Bible warns against other strange doctrines.

Some examples include:
Doctrine of men Matthew 15:7-9; Colossians 2:8
Doctrine of Balaam Revelations 2: 14; 2 Peter 2:1-3
Doctrine of the devil (demons) 1 Timothy 4:1&2
Doctrine of the World Colossians 2:8, 20-23
Doctrine of native culture Romans 12:1&2
You are encouraged to abide in the doctrine of Christ 2 John 9&10
Accept His Standards Matthew 5:7; John 13:16
I am with you even to the end; Matthew 28:20
I am coming back to take you home John 14:1-4
Ask and you shall receive John 14:12&13; Matthew 7:7

Do not worry about tomorrow Luke 12:26, 29; Philippians 4:6
I am the Lord who heals you of sicknesses Mark 5-8
Believe and entrust your whole being to Jesus. He is able to stand by you until the very end of the journey of life. Luke 10:1-6, 17; Matthew 6:24-34; John 15:1-8; Hebrews 13:5-6; Hebrews 11:1&2, 6

Course 2: What will YOU have me do, Lord?

Saul was a native of Tarsus, a citizen of Rome. He was zealous after the order of the Pharisees and teachers of the Jewish tradition. He got converted on the way to Damascus and was asked why he persecuted the Church. His response was "Lord who are you? What would YOU have me suffer for your sake?" Acts 9:1-6

This question relates to us as workers and we can draw a code of conduct from it.

It is an act of submission 1 Peter 2:13-25; Ephesians 6:5-9; Titus 2:9&10; 3:1

It is an act of willingness to do the work Acts 9:20; John 10:17-19; 1 Corinthians 9:18&19

It is an act of a heart's accent to responsibility and accountability Acts 9:16; John 10:13-18; 14:12; 5:20

It is a willingness to obey instructions from higher authorities Deuteronomy 31:7&8; John 12:49, 50; Isaiah 30:21

Course 3: I love my Lord so I must work the work

The Lord Jesus Christ is our perfect example. He is our lover because while we were yet in sin, Christ died for us. Ephesians 2:1-4; 1 Corinthians 5:15. Arising from this thought, I hereby oblige.

It is a sign-on and a sign-up to commitment, a commitment of a life time of serving Jesus Christ. 1 Corinthians 15:58; Colossians 3:22-25; Matthew 25:14-30

It is an expression of faithfulness and loyalty. John 8:28&29

No selfish ambitions John 6:38; Colossians 3:17; Matthew 7:18; John 12:49&50

No eye service Matthew 25:45-51;

No deceit Matthew 21:28-32

No divide and rule or sowing seed of disunity Proverbs 6:16-19

It is recognizing constituted authority. John 8:28, 29; 1 Timothy 6:1&2

It is being available spending time in doing the work. Ecclesiastes 3:1-9

Make yourself available

Make yourself relevant at all time

Promptly do the work. 2 Timothy 4:1-5; Colossians 4:17

Course 4: I am a part of His family so I must finish the work

A worker who is committed should be able to endure and complete his / her assignment. His/Her mission ought to have an inspiration; that is something that influences him / her and must keep a tab and absolute gaze on the goal. Take a look at John 4:34.
It is an expression of determination
He knew he must finish the work John 5:36
He fixed His gaze on the task Luke 9:51
He knew the importance of time towards finishing the work so He would not misuse precious time in partying or picnic John 4:34&35; Philippians 3:12-15
It is an expression of diligence

A) An act of being careful to preserve and carry out a given task or duty towards a desired goal (1 Corinthians 9:19-21) Paul illustrates the principle that if one fails to exercise self control, self denial and love to others, he will not be able to accomplish his goal. He renounces his rights out of conviction of others first, so that his ministry is not limited. He realizes that he must maintain a good conscience and love towards them.

B) Diligence is an act of fixing one's mind to overcome in the midst of opposition and fear. (Acts 20:22-24) Paul's concerns...was it...preserving his life? OR; to finish or complete the work which God gave him? That Christ be magnified in his body; in life or in death Philippians 1:20&21

C) Diligence: obtaining a reward towards a completed task; persevering to the end (Proverbs 13:4; 22:29; 21:5). Great rewards are waiting for the faithful. Revelations 2:7, 11, 17, 26-28; 3:5, 12, 21

It is an expression of Patience Hebrews 12:1&2

To finish well, the work must be done with patience. This means that there must a virtue of perseverance and endurance. Hebrews 10:36; 6:11&12

You can touch the finish line. Philippians 4:13

The Lord Jesus endured and finished it on the cross John 17:4; 19:30

Paul endured and completed the race and his work for the Lord. 2 Timothy 4:7&8

You too can finish it if you fight a good fight. Luke 9:62; Hebrews 10:38&39

Count the cost, because you will not want to start what you cannot finish, God is waiting for you with resources (grace, strength and encouragement) to engage, perform and finish your task. What is worth doing at all is worth doing well.

Course 5: The enemy is not happy, so I am engaged in a fight

To engage in a fight means that we are in combatant war, not with fellow men or physical objects, but with spiritual beings. We are in constant war contending for the faith, for an expression of victorious Christian living and for the preservation of our souls against influences and offense. We war against the following:

The Flesh: the corrupt desires within us (the sinful nature) Romans 7:7-25
The World: the ungodly pleasures of this world; their traditions and culture; their new introductions and philosophies. Matthew 13:22, 1 John 2:15-17; Colossians 2:8

Satan and his demons: these are powers of darkness who pose as spiritual rulers of the world; they energize the ungodly and oppose God's will and frequently attack believers of every age. (1 Peter 5:8-10; Psalm 22:13; Ezekiel 22:25)

1. The Flesh (Romans 7:4-25; 8:5-14; 6:11-19; Galatians 5:16-21)
Paul explains what FLESH is:

- That corrupt desire within us, which in time past believers obeyed in ignorance.
- Sinful nature struggling to gain control whereby holding a believer captive; to obey, resulting to sin. (v9-13)
- The conflict or battle in the soul. The believer is struggling within him to either yield to the desire of the Holy Spirit or that of the flesh. The mind (soul) is the battleground and

usually expressed in the will-power to act. The power to say no to the flesh is in your thought (your will-power) Proverbs 23:7; Isaiah 26:3; Romans 16:19. You can be retarded to sin in your thought!

Remedy
Through the power of the Holy Spirit we can put to death Mr. Flesh (Romans 8:4&5, 13&14). To live after the flesh is to live after "the sinful elements of human nature." It is to have or hold the desire to indulge in pleasure of sin; be occupied with and gratify the corrupt desire of sinful human nature. Read Galatians 5:19-21. You can tame your thoughts and desires! You can be allergic and offensive to accepting the world's standards contrary to decent and modest living. Such things as obscenity, pornography, drug addictions, mental and emotional low esteems, pleasures from sensual talks and such like disorders should really make you sick as a Christian worker.

Note:
1. It is impossible to follow after the flesh and the Holy Spirit at the same time. If anyone fails to live by the Spirit, (lives according to the flesh), he becomes an enemy of God and is spiritually dead. (Romans 8:13)

2. Our spiritual warfare, though often directed against Satan and evil forces, should primarily be against the passions and desires of the flesh, the sinful nature.

3. There should be a conscious decision and declaration to surrender to the will of God (2 Peter 1:4; Romans 6:13)

By receiving and following the Spirit we are delivered from the power of sin and are led onward to final glory in Christ.

This experience is the normal Christian life under the full provision of the gospel and daily adherence to scriptural teachings.

There are many in the Church today who acknowledge the righteousness, purity, and excellence of the gospel of Christ, yet because they have not experienced the regenerating grace of Christ (wearing religious garbs) find themselves in bondage of sin, slavery and immorality. Such people need a soul purge!

The unregenerate person maintains a losing conflict against sin and is at last taken captive. Sin finally triumphs and the person is sold as a slave to it. (Romans 7:15-19; 6:12, 16)

Failure to put to death the sinful nature (Mr. FLESH) of the body leads to spiritual death and a loss of inheritance in the kingdom of God (Galatians 5:21)

Life without the grace of Christ is a life of defeat, misery and bondage to sin. Spiritual life, freedom from condemnation, victory over sin and fellowship with God come through the union with Jesus Christ by the indwelling Holy Spirit.

2. The World (1 John 2:15-17)

The term "WORLD" refers to the cosmos; the vast system of this age which Satan promotes; exists independent of God. It consists not only in the obvious evil, immoral and sinful pleasures of the system but refers to a spirit of rebellion, resistance or indifference to God and His revelation that exists within all human enterprises that are not under the Lordship of Jesus Christ. The WORLD also includes all manmade religious systems and all unbiblical, spiritually deficient organizations and /or political or trade establishments. The world and the true Church are two distinct group entities. The world is under the dominion of Satan (John 12:31) and the Church belongs exclusively to God. (Revelations 21:2; Ephesians 5:23&24) In the world, believers are pilgrims and strangers. We are a nation within nations (Hebrews 11:13; 1 Peter 2:11). Satan, being in control, has organized the world into political, cultural, economic and religious systems that are hostile towards God and His people. (John 7:7; 15:18; 1 John 2:16-18) These refuse and refute the truth from the believer.

From the world, true Christians experience tribulations (John 16:2&3); hatred (John 15:9);

persecution (Matthew 5:10-12); and suffering (Romans 8:22&23; 1 Peter 2:19-29). Loving the world defiles our fellowship with God and leads to spiritual destruction. It is impossible to love the world and the Father at the same time. (Matthew 6:24)

To love the world means being in intimate fellowship with and devotion to its values, interest, ways and pleasures. It means taking pleasure in or enjoying in what is offensive and opposed to God (Luke 23:35). Therefore as believers we must come out of the world (John 15:19) not to be conformed to the worldly system (Romans 12:2; 1John 2:15); hate the worldly philosophy (Hebrews 1:9); die to the world (Galatians 6:14) and be delivered from the worldly suggestions (Colossians 1: 13, 14). Believers must have no close or intimate fellowship with those who participate in the world's evil system; must be the light and salt to them (Matthew 5:13&14); must love them and attempt to win them to Christ (Mark 16:5; Jude 22&23).

3. Satan (Ephesians 6:10-18; 1 Peter 5:8-10; 2 Corinthians 10:3-15)

Christians face spiritual conflicts with Satan and a host of evil spirits (Matthew 4:10) These powers of darkness are the spiritual rulers of the world (John 12:31, 2 Corinthians 4:4) who energizes the ungodly (Ephesians 2:2), oppose God's will

(Matthew 13:38&39) and frequently attack believers of this age. (1 Peter 5:8). They constitute a vast multitude (Revelations 12:4, 7) and are organized into a highly systematized empire of evil with ranks and order (Ephesians 2:2; John 14:30)

Satan remains a threat to believers (Psalm 22:13; Ezekiel 22:25) and seeks to destroy them, especially through experiences of suffering (1 Peter 5:8&9) and poverty. Christians must wage war against all evil with the power of the Holy Spirit (2 Corinthians 10:3-5; Ephesians 6:10-18). Our victory has been secured by Christ Jesus himself through His death on the cross. (Colossians 1:13&14; 2:15; Ephesians 4:8; 1:7) We should access our victory by faith as we pray in the Holy Ghost. In our warfare of faith, we must endure hardships as good soldiers of Christ. (2 Timothy 2:3) and persevere (Ephesians 6:18).

Conclusion:

Consider the Christian life as a "a good fight of faith." This fight involves fighting against Satan (Ephesians 6:12); Paganism and spiritual insurgence (2 Timothy 3:1-5; Romans 1:21-32; Galatians 5:19-21); Immorality (2 Timothy 3:5; 4:3; 1 Corinthians 5:1); False teachers (2 Timothy 4:3-5; Acts 20:28-31); Distortion of truth (Galatians 1:6-12); Worldliness (Romans 12:2) and Sin (Romans 6:8-13; 1 Corinthians 9:24-27)

You must finish your work amidst trials, difficulties and temptations while remaining faithful to the Lord and Savior of your life (Hebrews 10:13; 2 Timothy 2:12; Hebrews12:1&2)

You must keep the faith in times of severe testing, discouragement and much affliction. Never compromise the truth of the gospel (2 Timothy 1:13, 14; 2:2; 3:14-16; 1 Timothy 6:12). Know that when the roll call will be made, God's approval will be handed to you: "the crown of righteousness" and many other crowns you would have earned as a result of your stewardship. God has reserved in heaven, rewards for all those who will keep the faith in righteousness (Matthew 19:27-29; 2 Corinthians 5:10; 2:17, 26; Revelations 3:5,12, 21)

Course 6: Got the sword and the word; I must make an impact

The invitation into the presence of God is not a one-time or sporadic visit. It is a lifetime thing; a call to live there and be sufficiently drowned in the rivers of living waters and lost in the presence of God. From Matthew 25:1-13, what is the state of servants of God who are dry of anointing? What are the traits of a minister who worships from afar? (Mark 14:54; Exodus 24:9-12; Jeremiah 23:25-30). What are the likely evidences of a man who dwells in God's presence? (Exodus 24:12; 1 Kings 17:1-5, 8; 2 Timothy 3:16-17; Romans1:16, 28).

There must be a standing in His presence before we can think of a Mount Carmel experience. The glory of His presence reveals itself. It purifies the heart and separates us from the world. It commissions us to serve (Isaiah 6:1-10; Exodus 34; 29-35; Matthew 17:1-3; 2 Peter 1:16-18).

Made in the Place of Prayer
Closely related to the presence of God in the life of a servant of God is the place of prayer. It is an important place in the making of a worker or a minister. Consider these Scriptures: Luke 3:21&22; Acts 9:11, 12, 17-19; 1 Chronicles 4:9-10; 2 Chronicles 1:7-12; Luke 1:13

How does prayer make a man of God? Some folks get involved in the place of prayer. Find out who these personalities are from Luke 22:40-44; Romans 8:26; and Hebrews 7:25-27. Real prayers that aim at results and make an impact on men's lives and thus have relevance in God's programs are not piecemeal prayers. They are prayers that affect people and are potent enough to show the power of the Most High

Prayer pits two wills against each other: God's will and man's will. Most often, God's will prevails. The servant of God stands as a priest on behalf of the people (Exodus 28:1-25; 1 Peter 2:7-10; Colossians 1:16-28). The purpose of God for your

calling is not for any show or shame but for the following reasons:
to show forth His glory and beauty in a mortal vessel; to present every man perfect before Christ Jesus at His appearing and to teach and demonstrate the power of God to principalities and powers of darkness

You are made in your Study Room
"Search the Scriptures, for in them you think you have life, they are which speak of me" (John 5:39; 2 Timothy 2:15). Faith comes by hearing (listening to or reading and studying) the Word of God. Faith is shaped and empowered by knowledge and doctrine. The parchments are still needed in today's ministry, and you need to be equipped with the right tools and knowledge before you dive into ministry or enlist into working for God!

WATCH AND PRAY
Believers need to guard themselves carefully against heretics (Titus 3:9-11). Heretics are false teachers who teach opinions and doctrines that have no Biblical basis. They creep into Church to create division and cart away your money. The Lord Jesus Christ warned His disciples thirteen times in the gospels to be aware of leaders who would mislead (Matthew 7:15; 16:6,11; 24:4,24; Mark 4:24; 8:15;

12:38-40; 13:5; Luke 12:1; 17:23; 20:46; 21:8; 2 Peter 2:1-3)
Examine the teachers / leaders lest you fall with them. (1 Thessalonians 5:21; 1 John 4:1; 2 Peter 2:12-22; 2 Timothy 4:1-5). Paul warned of it too. (2 Corinthian 11:1-15). All professing Christians should examine themselves to ascertain that their salvation is a present reality. (2 Corinthians 13:5)

Second, believers need to maintain more interest in the second coming of the Lord Jesus Christ than any other thing. (Matt. 25:13; Mark 13: 32-37). Are you ready for the second coming of the Lord Jesus Christ?

Course 7: My work will be tested
Revelation 1:17-20; 2:1-29; 3:1-22
"I know your works" What does this mean to us? What does it imply in the context of all we have been learning during this training; two main things it can imply are
1) Someone is keeping watch over you (Matthew 16:27)
2) The person watching over you is also keeping records of your activities, good and bad.
> However, what should strike us most when we read Revelations 2&3 are the messages sent to the seven different churches by the Record Keeper; our Savior and Lord Jesus Christ and

the relevance of the messages for Churches today.
➢ The relevance of the messages for Churches today include:

1) A revelation of what Jesus Christ Himself loves and values in His Churches as well as what He hates and condemns
2) A clear statement from Christ regarding the consequences of disobedience and spiritual neglect and the rewards for spiritual vigilance and faithfulness to Christ.
3) A standard by which any Church or individual may judge his or her true spiritual state before God
4) An example of the methods that Satan uses to attack the church or the individual Christian
5) An emphasis on the fact that the Lord Jesus Christ is coming back and His desire to meet with overcomers
- Each of these revelations can be discussed in details with references to:

1) How does Christ's love, value or praise affect your life?
2). How does His love, values and praises affect a Church?
- For not bearing with evil persons. Revelation 2:2

- For testing the life, doctrine and claims of Christian leaders. Revelation 2:2
- For persevering in faith, love witness, service and suffering for Christ. Revelation 2:3, 10, 13, 19, 26
- For hating what God hates, Revelation 2:6
- For overcoming sin, Satan, and the ungodly world (Revelation 2:7, 11, 17, 26; 3:5, 12, 21)
- For refusing to conform to immorality in the world and worldliness in the Church. Revelation 2:24; 3:4
- For keeping the Word of God. Revelation 3:8, 10) What does Christ condemn?
- For failing to maintain a close personal relationship to Himself and God. Revelation 2:4
- For departing from biblical faith. Revelation 2:24-25
- For becoming spiritually dead Revelation 3:1
- For becoming spiritually lukewarm Revelation 3:15-16
- For substituting outward success and affluence for real spirituality i.e. purity, righteousness and spiritual wisdom. Revelation 3:17-18

How does Christ punish Churches that decline spiritually and tolerate immorality within their midst? He punishes such churches by

- By removing them from their place of grace in the Kingdom of God (Revelation 2:5; 3:16)
- By turning them away from the presence of God (fullness of joy), the genuine power of the Holy Spirit, the true biblical message of salvation, and the protection of their members from Satan's destruction (Revelation 2:5, 16, 22-23, 3:16)
- By placing their leaders under the judgment of God (Revelation 2:20-23)

How does Christ reward Churches that persevere and remain loyal to Him and His word? He rewards such Churches by:
- By delivering them from temptation (or trial) that will come upon the whole world. Revelation 3:10
- By giving them His love, presence and close fellowship. Revelation 3:20
- By blessing them with eternal life with God. Revelation 2:11, 17, 26; 3:5, 12; 21:7

Course 8: I've made a decision to be a team player
Consider the 12 apostles:
1. Peter: (Greek: Petros meaning 'Rock'): Jesus gave him a name 'Cephas', an Aramaic name. John translated it into Greek 'Petros' meaning Rock. (John 1:42 - "you will be called Cephas.") Peter was a

native of Bethsaida (John 1:44), was the brother of Andrew, lived in a fishing town- Capernaum. (Mark 1:29) He was a fisherman by profession at the Sea of Galilee. He was a married man. (Mark 1:30, 1 Corinthians 9:5)

2. John: (Meaning – God is gracious) John was originally the disciple of John the Baptist (John 1:35), a fisherman

3. James: (Greek Iakobos– the English word for Jacob or he who supplants his Brother). James was the son of Zebedee (Mark 4:21), the older brother of John (Matthew 17:1), by profession a fisherman

4. Andrew: (Greek –Andreas, meaning 'Manly', man), was the brother of Simon Peter, the son of Jonas, lived in Capernaum like his brother, and was a fisherman by profession. He brought Peter, his brother, to Jesus. (John 1:25-42)

5. Philip: (Greek – Philippos, meaning 'Lover of horses'). He was a close friend of Andrew and Peter, and a native of Bethsaida (John 1:44). Jesus called Philip near Bethany where John the 6. Baptist was preaching (John 1:43). He was the one who persuaded and brought Nathaniel to Jesus. (John 1:45-51)

6. Bartholomew: (Greek –Bartholomaios meaning Son of Talmai). He is mentioned in all the four lists of the apostles in the New Testament. There is no other reference to him in the New Testament. Nothing much is known about him.

7. Thomas: (Greek -Thomas from Aramaic - te'oma meaning 'twin') He is also called 'Didymus' or 'the Twin' (John 11:16, 20:24, 21:2). Profession is unknown

8. Matthew: (Greek -Maththaios- meaning 'gift of Yahweh') is also called 'Levi' (Mark 2:14, Luke 5:27). He was a tax collector by profession. Jesus called him to be one of his disciples, when he was at the tax office (Matthew 9:9, Mark 2:14)

9. James: He was one of the apostles of Christ. He was the son of Alphaeus.. Nothing much is known about him.

10. Thaddaeus: He is mentioned in two of the four lists of Jesus' disciples. (Matthew 10:3, Mark 3:18). In the other two lists he is variously called as Jude of James, Jude Thaddaeus, Judas Thaddaeus or Lebbaeus. Nothing else is known about him apart from the mention of his names in the two lists.

11. Simon the Zealot: He is another disciple of Jesus. He was a member of a party later called as the 'Zealots' (Matthew 10:4, Mark 3:18)

12. Judas Iscariot: He is the disciple who betrayed Jesus. His last name 'Iscariot' is from the Hebrew word 'Ish Kerioth' meaning 'a man from Kerioth', a place in the south of Judah (Joshua 15:25). He was a treasurer of the group. (John 12:6; 13:29). After his betrayal of Jesus, he grieved for his actions and committed suicide (Matthew 27:5). He is always mentioned last in the list of apostles.

FOR CLASS DISCUSSION:

Can you differentiate among their temperaments given their occupations?

How was Jesus able to handle or coordinate 'a zealot' and a 'tax collector'?

What do say of the 'talking Peter' and 'a reserved Andrew' How did they work together?

What are the methods we may employ in handling conflicts? (Conflict Resolutions)

Given divers cultural mix of the Church, what can a worker do to bring unity among brethren?

When you hear a 'story' about someone else or about the leadership of the Church, what remedies do you use to stop the circulation of falsehood?

How do you improve (as a person) on the process of Church governance?

Course 9: My expectation will not be cut off, there's a pay day!

He is a joint heir with Jesus Christ. (Differentiate between joint heir and co-heir). When God said we are joint heirs with Jesus, it means everything that God has is ours and whatever Jesus claims for Himself we can also claim. He is friend of Jesus. John 15:15; He has shown everything he learnt from Father to us. Hence a disciple must be a friend of His Master. You will no longer be treated as stranger in the house of God.

You are now given the permission to draw near to God. Hebrews 10:19-22.

Course 10: My DEPARTMENT'S JOB DESCRIPTION: I'm set to go!

Bible Study Group: Prepare & teach Sunday School; Organize teaching workshops / seminars; Teach Home Cells; Coordinate the approved material for use at different Natural Group meetings and Departments.

Prayer Department: Lead prayer sessions; intercede for the Church; Organize prayer seminars / workshop / special prayer events; Teach on how to pray; Coordinate prayer cells; Position at the spiritual watch tower of the Church and call for spiritual engagement.

Children's Church: Prepare & Teach the children; organize VBS; Take kids on tour and picnics; Prepare kids for events; Keep classrooms clean; Mentor & care for kids; Organize concerts, special events for kids; Organize grand parents' day.

Choir: Write, Prepare & Present songs at every Church service; Ensure spiritual aura and impact on every worship or teaching service; Keep the altar holy and clean always; Form an excellent image of the Church from the altar; Appear with clean, moderate matching attire; Lifting hearts up to the Lord Jesus Christ with worship songs and hymns. Teach Church new songs, at least one per month. Present a quarterly report to the Pastor.

Ushers: Constitute cheerful greeters at Church entrance; Maintain orderly sitting in Church; Conduct traffic flow of vehicles outside; Maintain order during worship service; Collate all monies from tithe & offerings & building funds same day and submit same to Finance Dept.; Form an excellent image of the Church with clean matching attire.

Evangelism, Visit and Follow up:
See to members welfare; Welcome new attendees; Call, encourage members; Follow up new converts; Organize picnics; Food Drives; Back to School Drives; Homeless People's visits; Organize evangelism efforts; Advertise programs, Provide the 'Dominion Welcome" to invited guests and Church members.

Training: Organize training sessions for spiritual growth; professional advancement; Prepare, present Believers' Class & Workers Training in collaboration with Pastor, Coordinate School of Disciples; Organize seminars & workshops

Sanitation: Clean, sanitize Church, bathrooms and classrooms regularly; Buff Church floor; Rake leaves and maintain cleanliness at outside perimeter; Organize the altar and do Decorations where necessary; Maintain overall cleanliness of the Church.

Maintenance: Fix or arrange for contractors to fix broken infrastructure of building; Be handy to fix expedient leaks, breaks, and failing systems; Liaise with Pastor to maintain general regulatory procedures for the facility; Work with Men Group to mow lawns, snow & rake leaves at outside perimeter; Maintain facility for outdoor events; Coordinate vendor submissions. Present quarterly reports to Pastor.

Media & Security: Maintain quality production of audio output; produce audio visuals, CDs, DVDs; Manage and maintain Church website; In collaboration with Administrative office, provide social media content and delivery system for Church communication purposes only. Responsible for advertisement of programs and events; Maintain security networks and organizing. Work in collaboration with Choir Director for Church equipment updates, maintenance and supplies.

Finance: Prepare annual Church account; Collate all contributions and provide such to Pastor; Collate all receipts for income & expenditure financial reporting; Prepare Balance Sheet for the Church; Advise on balances on account before expenses are approved.

Administration: Write letters, collate minutes of meetings; Log member directory; Maintain Church & Pastor's Office protocols; Duals as Public Relations Officer of Church; Keep inventories; memories, artifacts and memoirs. Advises Pastor on administrative processes

Teens NATURAL GROUP: Promote spirituality and success in academics through Teens engagement and participation in activities: Picnics, Bible Quiz, Games, Fund Raising, Educational Trips; Foster Teen Integration and Competitions.

Young Adults NATURAL GROUP: Promote spirituality and success in academics through Peer engagement and participation in activities, Picnics, Bible Quiz, Games, Fund Raising, Trips Marriage Seminars; Home & Family Startup Events, Professional Training Events; Community Initiatives and Involvement; Support Men's Group in keeping Church infrastructure, etc.

Women NATURAL GROUP: Married women who promote spirituality, family life, professionalism, home care and children & husband welfare by engaging in and supporting nursing mothers with new babies, conducting Baby Showers for expectant mothers, and organizing wake keeping / service of songs for; or visiting bereaved members. Organize food for Family Week event; Founders' Day (Anniversary) and Vacation Bible School.

Men's NATURAL GROUP: Married men who promote spirituality, family life, professionalism, home care and children & wives' welfare and Church sustainability by engaging in and supporting men without jobs or new to society; organizing professional training and business start ups; wake keeping / service of songs for bereaved members. Provide foods and drinks for Family Week event; Founders' Day (Anniversary) and Vacation Bible School. Support Elders and Pastor in Church governance.

REFERENCES

1. Christ Redeemers Ministries "School of Disciples" Year One through Year Ten Booklets. Lagos Nigeria, 1988. http://www.rccg.org or http://www.rccgna.org

2. Scripture Union Nigeria Bible Study series 1980-2000

3. Nigerian Fellowship of Evangelical Students training manuals 1980 through 1987, University og Nigeria Nsukka, Nigeria

4. Sermon Notes from RCCG Dominion Center, Cincinnati Ohio http://www.dominioncenter.us.

5. Scott, Francis; The Star Spangled Banner Lyrics: http://www.usa-flag-site.org/song-lyrics/star-spangled-banner.shtml

6. TheAmplifiedBible;Copyright©1954,1958,1962,1964,1965, 1987 by The Lockman Foundation

7. The National Anthem

8. Martin Luther King Jr.(Quotes)

9. Isaac Watts (The Soldier I am: Song) http://www.churchhymnal.org

10. Bee Illustrated "The Soldier at Heart"

11. Onward Christian Soldier (Song) http://www.churchhymnal.org

12. Three Stages of Production & The Production Function; Numerical Example: Lecture Notes from Emory University 13. Business School; MEMBA Class. http://www.emory.bus.edu

13. The Ear & Goat (Ruminants) ADAM Pictures

    http://www.adam.com

14. Jim Elliott Quotes (missionary to Ecuador)

15. C. T. Studd; "No Retreat" 1958. Youth With A Mission Publishers (an inspiring true story of men and women who answered the call of God

16. Emmanuel Elendu 2015 "Digging For Gold" WestBow Publishing, a Division of Thomas Nelson Publishers, Wilmington Bloomberg, Indiana USA.

OTHER BOOKS BY EMMANUEL ELENDU

1. Commodity Map of Nigeria
2. Before You Quit
3. Digging for Gold
4. Anatomy of the Virgin Birth

In the Press... out in 2017
1. Discipleship in the Digital Age
2. Sounds, Echoes & Fury

www.ingramcontent.com/pod-product-compliance
Lightning Source LLC
LaVergne TN
LVHW051606070426
835507LV00021B/2790